THE TECHNIQUES OF
BASKETRY

VIRGINIA I. HARVEY

UNIVERSITY OF WASHINGTON PRESS

Seattle and London

Anita Fechter's handsome sculptural basket is sterling-silver wire worked in a coiling technique (see figure 3-51). Three seashells from the Philippine Islands enhance the design, which won an honorable mention in the 1971–1972 Sterling Silver Design Competition sponsored by the Sterling Silversmith's Guild, Riverside, Connecticut. 10" long x 10" wide x 8" high.

To my mother, with gratitude for her encouragement, guidance, and companionship

By the same author:

Macramé: The Art of Creative Knotting
Color and Design in Macramé
Weft Twining (Harriet Tidball, coauthor)
Threads in Action (a quarterly publication, 1969–1974)
Split-ply Twining
Multiple Tabby Weaves
Bateman Blend Weaves
Park Weaves

University of Washington Press edition first published 1986

Front cover: "Sunrise, The Birth of Morning," by Larry Metcalf (36" × 72" × 6"; linen, wool, and rayon; twining, with some Ghiordes knots). *Back cover* (left to right): basketry sculpture by Arrowmont student; wall hanging by Naoko Furue; coiling by L. Coutts; basket by Harlene Anthony.

Library of Congress Cataloging-in-Publication Data

Harvey, Virginia I.
  The techniques of basketry.

  Bibliography: p.
  Includes index.
  1. Basket making. I. Title. II. Title: Basketry.
[TT879.B3H38 1986]   746.41'2   86–19057
ISBN 0–295–96415–4 (pbk.)

CONTENTS

ACKNOWLEDGMENTS

It is surprising how many people have basketry collections, or, if they don't, they uncover interesting baskets in antique shops, flea markets, auctions, little-known museums, and many other places, including the homes of their friends. The quest has been too widespread to thank everyone who has helped. We all had fun, and perhaps that is thanks enough.

A special note of appreciation goes to Dr. Phillip Gifford, Department of Anthropology of the American Museum of Natural History in New York, for making it possible to study the Museum's vast collection of baskets and to photograph selected pieces.

Another thank-you goes to Miss Jean Mailey, who drew my attention to the Japanese baskets at the Metropolitan Museum of Art in New York.

An exhibition of historic and contemporary basketry at the San Fernando Valley State College, California, during the "Fibers" conference was the inspiration for this book. Professor Mary Ann Glantz of that college has inspired her students to create some extraordinary pieces. Her help in arranging to photograph her students' work was invaluable. Helen Richards has been teaching basketry as well as other textile techniques in the Los Angeles area, and she was very generous in sending me basketry pieces from her students and friends for study and for photographing. Despite many demands on their time, both of these talented and inspiring teachers have made valuable contributions to this book. Their help is deeply appreciated.

Ann Meerkerk spent many hours helping to solve the puzzles of some of the more complex plaiting patterns. That was fun too, but the opportunity to discuss the problems with someone else was appreciated. She also humanized figures 2-7 and 2-8 by giving them the appearance of some early people. In her words, "They are not identifiable as any particular tribe; rather, they look as though they had been assembled by a committee."

To Jean Tillman and Gertrude Hansen, owners of Casa de las Tejedoras, a weaving-supply shop in Santa Ana, California, a special note of appreciation. Despite the demands of their busy schedules, they gathered and shipped many of their own contemporary basketry pieces and others made by students at their shop for me to study and photograph.

Vivanna Phillips, another neighbor and good friend, made samples and tested materials and techniques.

Both Ed Rossbach and Peter Collingwood suggested references unknown to me that were helpful.

Lin Longpre, director of The Factory of Visual Art in Seattle, made space available for the workshop on basketry techniques that was a testing ground for the directions in the text. The class was composed of an exceptional group of people, and they contributed much to this work.

Some of the more unusual pieces that Leslie and Fred Hart purchased for their exceptional store in Seattle, La Tienda, found their way into the Harts' private collection of artifacts, textiles, and costume. They were generous in allowing me to study and to photograph their pieces.

Joan Walker's careful draftsmanship in executing the final drawings also contributed to the book.

As in all my publications, William Eng's photographs are vitally important. Without the benefit of his skill, much of the value of the book would be lost.

Last, and most important, a public thank-you added to many personal ones to Bill, my husband, for picking up all the loose ends I leave scattered behind me, and for ignoring those that neither one of us has time to catch.

Many people have taken valuable time to share in the production of this book. If it serves as a useful reference on the techniques of basketry, the time will have been well spent, and my appreciation will be the least important of their rewards. Good references are needed and wanted by craftsmen today, and when they are available, they are used and appreciated — the greatest reward possible for an author and for those who have helped her.

PREFACE

Basketry is such a vast and complex subject that it would take a series of publications equivalent to a small set of encyclopedias to cover it adequately. One volume could be devoted to the history and the uses of basketry; another to the designs and their significance. A large book could be written on the identification of baskets. Just a listing of materials used throughout the world, their processing, and the cultures that used each material would fill another volume. A bibliography might not fill a book, but it certainly would take many pages. And if every technique were illustrated and explained, it would make a volume so large the cost would be prohibitive.

Baskets have played an important part in the lives of people from practically every culture and level of civilization. Even today, it is a rare household that does not have at least one basket, and usually several—some functional and some merely decorative.

Since they have been a part of man's life for so many centuries, it is natural that much has been written about them. Basketry was a popular subject for scholarly articles, monographs, and books among anthropologists during the latter part of the last century and the first half of the twentieth century. These scientists penetrated remote areas and documented the techniques carefully. Victorian needlework publications frequently included directions for various kinds of basketry, since all kinds of handwork were fashionable during that period. (In keeping with the styles of that time, the baskets were usually decorated with beads, tassels, feathers, or fringes, and the designs were elaborate in the extreme.) The basketry of the American Indians was also the subject of many excellent studies. Occasional books and articles have appeared since midtwentieth century, but generally they explain a few of the most common techniques, and many of them include specific directions for baskets of very conventional design, usually made with reeds.

A survey of the literature reveals that no single book covers all the techniques of all cultures, and this book is no exception. It is impossible to see every basket that has been made or to find and study all of the literature published on the subject. However, many months were spent on research to uncover as many techniques as possible, and the results are included here.

In order to document all of the important techniques that could be found, discussions of history, the significance of designs on baskets, and the traditional materials are kept to a minimum here. This text concentrates not on who did them or what was done by whom, but rather on how they were done.

No patterns for specific articles are included, and no directions for any of the pieces illustrated are available, but all of the techniques presented are illustrated and explained carefully. Many of the techniques are so simple that it is possible to "read" a picture of a basket and then reconstruct it.

Both historical and contemporary articles made with basketry techniques are illustrated to serve as inspiration. The book is meant to teach you these excellent old techniques so you can use them in pieces designed by you for today's lifestyle.

Since the first publication of this book, some progress in the standardizing of textile terminology has occurred. Specific terms are important to textile professionals who are documenting textiles and communicating with their colleagues. Also, the number of serious amateurs who wish to use exact terms is increasing.

Some of the terms used in this book no longer agree with the new definitions. For instance, *weaving* may no longer be used for the method of producing a basket. Certainly, in general use we still "weave a basket," because this phrase has been accepted for too long to disappear. However, when textile professionals communicate, all forms of the verb *to weave* may not be used for basketry.

In this edition, it is not possible to change *weave* or *woven* without rewriting much of the text. For the reader who needs to use precise terms, the most widely accepted reference at this time is Irene Emery's *The Primary Structures of Textiles.* Soon to be published is another important reference: *Interlacing: The Elemental Fabrics* by Jack Lenor Larsen.

At the end of the text explaining the Mad Weave (pages 94–96), step-by-step directions for moving this plaiting from horizontal to vertical have been added to this edition. A few other changes have been made: the index has been expanded, and errors have been corrected. Also, a few diagrams have been enlarged for clarity.

Interest in basketry has increased since the first publication of this book. Many other basketry books and some newsletters have been published, guilds have been formed, and classes and conferences have brought interested people together. Some have studied the techniques, and gathered and used traditional materials, to create traditional baskets. Others have applied the techniques to natural and man-made materials to achieve contemporary designs. Many beautiful traditional and contemporary objects have been produced, and I hope that the information in this book will be used for the creation of many more.

VIRGINIA I. HARVEY

BASKETRY – PAST AND PRESENT

A LONG HISTORY

Anthropologists, archeologists, and textile specialists seem to agree that basketry was practically universal among the ancient civilizations and that it was one of the earliest crafts, predating pottery and weaving. George Wharton James devoted a chapter of his book, *Indian Basketry,* to the thesis that it was the mother of pottery in the Americas. Prior to the publication of his book in 1903, he watched the Havasupi Indians line a shallow basket with a mixture of clay and sand to protect the basket when food and coals were placed together in it for cooking. Constant heating caused the clay lining to harden and separate from the basket, thus creating a piece of pottery. In fact, evidence has been found that, as early as 5000 B.C., Indians in New Mexico and Arizona were using baskets as molds for cooking pots, and pottery with impressions of basketry has been found in remnants of many other cultures. No doubt the discovery of this process led to the manufacture of other containers and utensils, so this seems a reasonable explanation of the beginnings of pottery. Even after pottery-making was divorced from the basket molds, many patterns used for decoration imitated the basketry impressions that occurred on earlier pieces.

Any opinion regarding the origins of basketry must be speculation, because the materials from which baskets are made survive only under ideal conditions. Moisture is the most damaging element, so it is logical that most of the evidence attesting to the existence of ancient basketry has been found in arid areas. In some damp areas, however, even though baskets have disappeared, proof of their existence remained in impressions left on clay or mud. In his book, *Basketwork Through The Ages,* H. H. Bobart mentions the discovery of coiled basketry linings that were used in granaries sunk in the sand in the Fayyum settlement of Egypt. They were placed in the Badarian period, 10,000 to 8000 B.C.

Remnants dating back to 7000 B.C. were found at the Danger cave site near Wendover, Utah, and mud impressions of basketry proved that it existed around 5270–4630 B.C. in Jarmo, Iran. Who knows whether some earlier society used baskets of which no evidence survives?

In primitive cultures, basketry has filled so many functions for man it seems logical to conclude that it sprang from one need in one group and an entirely different need in another. We can speculate that as soon as man started gathering food, he needed a container. A gourd or shell may have sufficed in the beginning, but soon he found that it was easier to transport his harvest by fastening the gourd to his person, or perhaps he needed to free his hands for gathering the food. Probably he constructed some kind of network of vines to hold the gourd, and this was the first step. Then he discovered that a closer mesh in the net would eliminate the need for another container, and thus he could reduce the weight he carried. Other improvements would eventually lead to the many forms of burden baskets and containers we know today.

An idea for a container may have developed from watching a bird build a nest. The Mohave Indians made a storage basket with a ring of arrowwood stalks tightly interwoven in the same manner as a bird's nest. After this granary was filled with several bushels of mesquite beans or corn, the top was sealed with mud to make it weatherproof.

Again, observations of animal behavior may have had an influence. Some fish construct shelters. Chimpanzees have been seen jumping and rolling on a plaything made of vines that had been twisted and "woven" into a basket form, and there is little doubt that it was made by the monkeys.

1-1. Burden baskets, such as this one from Kenya, North Borneo, have been used throughout the world (see figure 7–84). (Courtesy of the American Museum of Natural History, New York)

cient cultures. According to anthropologist Gene Weltfish, basketry has been used "as a key to cultural and physical relations of native groups, past and present." A question always arises when the same craft technique is found to exist at the same time in widely separated ancient societies. If there is evidence of communication between the people, it is likely that one learned from the other. If no evidence of contact exists, is it possible that both cultures developed the same technique simultaneously? Was it the result of the need for the article, the availability of suitable material, the ingenuity of man, or some combination of these stimuli?

It seems logical that an ingenious man who needed to cross a river might, after seeing a group of dry stalks of cane floating on the surface, tie enough of the stalks together to support his weight and thus float to the other side. Once the idea was born, refinements would follow naturally, and the reed boat might be the eventual product.

While duplications of technique and form certainly could have evolved independently, the startling similarities that have occurred in many parts of the world have generated much debate among the students of ancient cultures. For instance, basketry boats used in Egypt as early as the fifth century B.C. were similar to those used by the Incas when the Spaniards arrived. Indians of Peru and Bolivia still use tortora-reed boats today, so these craft must be a very satisfactory solution for water transportation to have survived in the same form for so long.

Other similar boats have been used in Europe, India, Africa, and Southeast Asia. Some variations result from differing local materials: the Britons covered the exterior of their boats with hide, while the Egyptians covered theirs with bitumen. In Southeast Asia a mixture of pitch, lime, and oil was sometimes used; in other cases cow dung mixed with coconut oil provided the waterproofing.

Although the techniques were similar, the size of the vessels varied. Very stable sea boats, some as large as fifty tons and carrying from one to three sails, were built by the natives of southern Indochina. They were used for one voyage a year, during the favorable monsoon, then were dismantled and stored until they were needed again.

Small, very light, graceful craft, rounded at both ends and wider at the stern than at the bow, were used as family boats in Indochina. Usually

The need to snare small game or trap fish may have been the first impetus. Many primitive societies have learned to make efficient traps with basketry techniques.

Protection from the elements is another basic human need, and it is a logical step from cutting palm branches and placing them on a support, one on top of the other, to intertwining and eventually plaiting the fronds to make a more secure shelter.

The development of basketry boats has been an area of particular interest and speculation for anthropologists and other students of an-they were no larger than twelve feet long and five feet wide, and four or five bamboo poles held the gunwales out, making the boat wide for its length and leaving little freeboard. In spite of their light, shallow structure, they could carry several passengers and their luggage. The frames of both the large vessels and the small boats were formed of very closely woven strips of bamboo.

As time passes, more facts concerning the travel of ancient peoples are uncovered. Reconstructions of ancient vessels, such as the Kon-Tiki, have made experimental voyages to investigate the possible extent of early travel and communication. Recently, evidence of communication between the Mediterranean city of Sidon and South America has been discovered, and this may explain the similarity of the Egyptian and Inca boats. Scientists have deciphered the message on a stone left on the coast of Brazil by sailors from Europe in 531 B.C. — two thousand years before Columbus arrived in the New World!

Another puzzle, still unexplained, is the duplication of both coiled and twined basketry techniques in the Swiss Lake dwellings and in areas occupied by American Indians.

USES OF BASKETRY

In his book, *Aboriginal Indian Basketry*, Otis Mason lists 116 ways that basketry was used by the American Indians — some very specific, such as papoose baskets or drinking cups, others more general, such as dress or fine art. In some cultures, the wealth of a family was gauged by the number and quality of their baskets, and occasionally baskets were used as a medium of exchange.

In relation to food alone, baskets have been used for gathering, carrying, storing, drying, milling, mixing, cooking, and serving. To obtain the food, fish and game traps, hunting fences, and quivers made of basketwork have been used. Particularly in warm climates, walls or partitions, roofs, floors, and doors have been made of basketry. Basketwork furnishings for the house include curtains, awnings, hammocks, storage containers for treasures and costumes, mats for the floor and for bedding, cradles, and other furniture. Furniture made with wicker or with

1-2. Coiling was used on a large scale to make this attractive chair from Mexico. 24" high.

other basketry techniques, such as the chair in figure 1-2, is still used in homes today.

Many articles of clothing have been and are still made with these techniques. Twining was the predominant method for capes, robes, and armor. The hats of the Nootka Indians of the West Coast of North America included some of the finest work of this tribe. Although much of the Indian footwear was made of hide, plaited and twined sandals were worn also. Sometimes belts were made of twining; others were plaited, such as the one from New Guinea shown in figure 1-4. Counterparts of

1-3. A type of basketry hat worn by Nootka men when they were at sea in their canoes. The Nootka tribe occupied the western side of Vancouver Island. (Drawing by Joy Cole. From Dr. Frank W. Lamb, *Indian Baskets of North America*)

these articles of clothing may be found in stores today — plaited hats from Panama, summer shoes of interwoven vegetal fibers or leather strips, and baskets designed for summer handbags.

For travel, basketry canoe covers, cushions, and saddlebags have been used, in addition to the boats and sails already mentioned. Small pony carts and baby buggies have had wickerwork bodies. Wicker suitcases were more popular in the past than they are today, but Mexican basketry suitcases are still available.

In many societies baskets have played a very important role in religious and ceremonial life — in dances, for washbowls, as prayer baskets, gifts, coffins, and cremation baskets. Often a basketmaker's finest work would be buried with her or burned in her pyre. (Basketry was exclusively the province of women in many societies.)

Drums and musical instruments, such as the dance rattle in figure 1-5, were not unusual, and baskets were used in games and gambling. Cages for insects, animals, or birds served a useful purpose. A cage of fireflies has been used for lighting, and the Chinese made cricket cages. Cradles,

1-4. A belt plaited over a bark foundation from Kup, New Guinea. Extra bark, still attached to the belt, was coiled in the center of it. 2¾" wide. (Courtesy of the American Museum of Natural History, New York)

1-5. Cameroon rattle made of split vines with circles of hide for bases (see figures 7-34 and 7-97). 7" high. (Courtesy of the American Museum of Natural History, New York)

1-6. Toys are spilling out of an unusual basket from Bangladesh (see figure 8-1). The little plaited dog in the center was made in India; the other toys are Ecuadorian. The basket is 14" in diameter. (Courtesy of Leslie and Fred Hart)

Space permits only a brief mention of some notable accounts of man's use of basketry. Remnants of Celtic wickerwork were found in the Glastonbury Lake Village excavations, and Roman records indicate that they may have been part of the wall of a hut. The shields that protected the

1-8. An unusual piece of basketry—snowshoes for oxen, from northern Japan. (Courtesy of Leslie and Fred Hart)

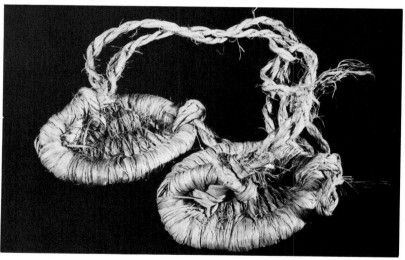

papoose baskets, and toys were made for the children. Toys like those in figure 1-6 from Ecuador and India are still being made today. Miniature baskets were made by American Indians, perhaps as toys, or maybe to demonstrate the skill of the basketmaker. Miniatures continue to challenge craftsmen today; the baskets shown in figure 1-7 are contemporary.

1-7. Miniature baskets made by Jean Tillman of brown, gray, blue, and natural wool. The largest one is 3" in diameter and 2½" high; the smallest is 1" in diameter and 1" high.

Britons from Caesar's invaders were made of basketry covered with hide, and other baskets made by the Britons were so highly prized by the Romans that they were used to hold offerings to their gods. Wealthy Roman citizens decorated their homes with beautiful and costly baskets, and evidence of wicker furniture appears in a Roman scene on a tombstone now in the Trier Museum in Germany.

Basketry has a continuous history in the British Isles, and there is still a Basketmakers Guild in London. As recently as 1937 a Royal Charter was

1-9. A nineteenth-century Japanese box that is an example of excellent design and meticulous craftsmanship. 7½" long × 4¾" wide × 4" high. (Courtesy of the Metropolitan Museum of Art, Bequest of Edward C. Moore, 1891)

granted to it by King George VI. Part of the duties of the warden of the Guild has been to inspect the production of all baskets in order to maintain a standard of good quality.

Contrary to the trend of many handicrafts during the Industrial Revolution, the demand for baskets increased. Baskets were used as containers for raw material and for many other purposes in the factories. Even as late as the Second World War, every basketmaker in England was kept busy filling an order for two million baskets to carry medical supplies for the British Army.

In European villages in the past, the basketmaker and his family grew and processed their willows, gathered rushes, wove the baskets, then carried them to market. Some families still carry on the tradition of weaving the baskets, but they now purchase their materials from others who cultivate the willows, and marketing methods also have changed.

In the area around Lichtenfels and Michelau in West Germany an active basketmaking industry still exists, and there is a State School of Basketry and a Basket Museum there. Baskets are made in state-controlled factories in East Germany and Poland, and willows are grown and exported from Poland, Bulgaria, and Yugoslavia, also under state control.

In the Orient plaiting and wickerwork have been the predominant techniques, and the interlacements developed for the former are the most complex to be found in basketry. These intricate methods, combined with the oriental elegance of design, attention to detail, and perfection of craftsmanship, even in the most delicate materials, have produced some of the most exquisite baskets in existence.

Containers play an important part in oriental tradition, particularly in China and Japan. Often the importance of a gift or the reverence for a work of art is expressed by the container selected for it. The packaging itself is a work of art, and frequently some form of basketry is used, so this tradition may have contributed to the beauty and complexity of their basketry.

American Indian baskets are renowned throughout the world for their beauty, their diversity of design and technique, and their long history. They were such an important part of the earliest identifiable southwestern culture that archeologists have designated that era as the "Basket-

maker Culture." Even in that prehistoric time, the baskets of the inhabitants of the region were notably fine. It is interesting to note that, according to Gene Weltfish, all basketry techniques used today in North America were practiced in the prehistoric cultures.

On the North American continent, the Aleuts have produced some of the most delicately twined pieces from beach grasses and a type of wild rye. Materials that were available in their barren and bleak land were very limited, so they used variations of the twining technique to introduce pattern into their work, frequently contrasting openwork with more compact twining. In later pieces, when other materials became available to them through trade, patterns were woven with an overlay technique, using dyed grasses or sometimes yarns of foreign manufacture.

In spite of the fact that many fine baskets were thrown into the fire and destroyed during part of the Feasts of the Dead ceremonies practiced by the Pomo Indians, enough of them survived to earn the Pomo women the reputation of being some of the most versatile and diversified of the world's basketmakers. Their baskets are beautiful in both form and design, remarkable for the fineness and evenness of their weave, and distinctive in color. They are usually a dull red, black, tan, or the brown of the pine root, except when colorful feathers are added to them. Shells were used in some of their older pieces. Some of their finer coiled baskets have thirty stitches per inch, and the finest may have as many as sixty coils to an inch. They have made exquisite little toys measuring no more than one-half inch in diameter.

The basketry of the West Coast and Southwest has been well documented; however, there is much less information on the eastern and midwestern Indians. Baskets were certainly a necessary part of the culture of the Plains and East Coast Indians, but they did not carry the craft to the high form that characterized western basketry. Techniques and materials that produce baskets more quickly, such as plaiting and wickerwork, and birchbark and splints, were more prevalent in the East and in the Great Lakes area. It is also very probable that European cultures had an important influence on these areas. This is not to say that there have been no noteworthy baskets, either ancient or modern, from the East and Midwest, but rather that in many instances the character of the work was quite different, and there was not the great proliferation of styles that occurred in the West.

COLLECTIONS AND CONSERVATION

As early as the turn of the century, collectors who realized the beauty and value of the American Indian baskets made some extensive collections. (Many of these have found their way into museums, and it is because of the foresight of these collectors that some fine specimens are on display and available for study today.) People are still collecting, even though old baskets are very costly now. The simple lines of the rooms and the natural wood backgrounds of contemporary architecture serve as an ideal setting for the beauty of fine pieces.

A few words about the care of baskets may be appropriate for those who have old ones they wish to preserve. Dirt and dust are the enemy of any natural fiber, so careful washing with warm water, mild soap, and a soft brush will help to preserve any basket made of vegetal fibers that is soiled. The basket should be rinsed thoroughly to remove all soap and placed where it will dry without undue delay.

If a basket is very old and brittle, it might be wise to place it in a humid place for a few days before handling it. Heat and dryness tend to make most basket materials brittle, so it is advisable to keep them away from heat registers and out of direct sunlight. On the other hand, any grasses

1-10. Robert Still, interior designer, displays baskets and other decorative objects among the books in his home. (Photograph by Sally Still)

and practically all wood substances will rot if they are kept wet for a period of time, so too much humidity is also damaging. A careful control of the moisture to keep the fibers from becoming extremely dry will prolong the life of any basket made of natural materials.

When an old piece is handled, a strain should never be placed on the delicate fibers. For instance, if the old material is brittle, a basket may break when it is picked up by the side. Instead, it should be cradled in the hands. Treat your choice old piece gently, keep it clean, and enjoy the beauty created by the incredibly patient basketmaker. No craftsman, ancient or modern, could wish for more than to have his work well preserved and cherished by its successive owners. In turn, collectors should feel an obligation to care for the pieces, and they should enjoy and treasure them.

BASKETRY TODAY

That basketry has survived at all is surprising. Practically every need that was filled by an object made of basketry in the past is satisfied by at least one manufactured article today. Cardboard and paper, metal and plastic are now used where baskets once functioned. For instance, Pima storage baskets have been replaced with fifty-gallon oil drums, and the traditional market basket has been replaced with paper bags.

Baskets are used today by choice rather than by necessity, and the multitude of them available for purchase is a measure of their popularity. In fact, if care is taken in selection, baskets can be one of the greatest bargains in folk art available today. They come from many parts of the world — inexpensive containers from Taiwan and the Philippines, colorful baskets from Mexico and Morocco, sturdy wickerwork from England, among others. In some instances native American Indian work can be found, usually in shops near where the basketmakers live and work. Small trinket baskets of twining with false embroidery made by the Makah Indians can be found in a few shops in the Northwest. Native baskets are available along the coast of the Carolinas, birchbark baskets decorated with porcupine quills can occasionally be found in the Midwest, and splint baskets in many sizes and shapes can be purchased in the Great Lakes region. No doubt, given the opportunity to search, native American baskets could be located in other areas.

The little-known story of the Nantucket baskets is interesting. Men who were stationed during the nineteenth century on the lightships that stood guard, sometimes for months at a time, on shoals around Nantucket made baskets to pass the time. They were open baskets (see figure 1-12), patterned after Indian baskets from the area, and they were used for everything from firewood to collecting eggs or holding clothespins. They came to be known as Nantucket Lightship baskets and are now collectors' items.

After the Second World War, José Formosa Reyes married a woman from Nantucket and moved there from the Philippines. He expected to obtain a teaching position, but when it did not materialize, he turned to basketry as an occupation. He designed and produced baskets similar to

1-12. A nest of baskets from Nantucket (see figures 2-10 and 5-4).

the Lightship baskets, but with lids. These baskets were used as hand-bags, and they have become very popular accessories for the residents of the island. His styles vary somewhat in shape and size, but never so much that they are not always recognizable as Nantucket baskets. Some of them have an ivory whale, gull, or dolphin mounted on the wood of the lid; others have an ivory oval with a scrimshaw design on it — frequently a picture of the owner's home on Nantucket (see figure 1-13). Other appointments may be ivory too, and the workmanship of the baskets is flawless. They are cherished and kept in fine repair, and they have become symbols of their owners' attachment to Nantucket. The average basketmaker can produce only one basket a week, and there are few basketmakers left. The number of people who are doing scrimshaw is also limited, so a genuine Nantucket basket is difficult to find and expensive.

Basketry is taking a new direction today. In the past, basketmakers worked almost entirely from the viewpoint that form follows function. A container was needed, so a piece was designed to fill this need. Decoration was included to make the piece more beautiful, but a basketry piece was seldom made for decoration only. Since craftsmen no longer have to confine their efforts to utilitarian articles, they are free to design without the limitations of function.

This new freedom is being extensively explored by craftsmen. Non-traditional materials are being coiled, twined, woven, and plaited into new forms and shapes. It is interesting to note that many articles retain the container structure, such as the small pothanger in figure 1-14. The materials that were used give it a modern look, and it will serve a useful purpose and add a colorful note to a room. A review of the contemporary pieces shown in this text will reveal many container-like designs; however, a few craftsmen have succeeded in developing new forms. A primarily decorative approach to basketry presents many challenges, and it will be interesting to watch the innovative craftsmen of today carry basketry to a new level of achievement.

1-13. A Nantucket basket made for Norma Minstrell by her coworkers at the Cobble Court Basket Shop. The scrimshaw was done by Nancy Chase. 7" long x 7" wide x 10" high (without handle).

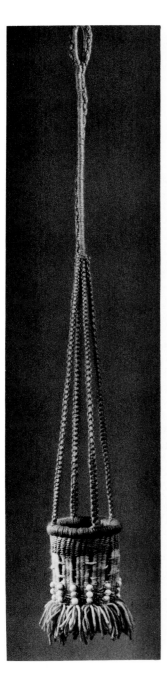

(Left) 1-14. A colorful pothanger in orange tones by Mieke Solari. It was twined over reeds with flax and rug wools. 48″ long x 5⅓″ wide.

(Right) 1-15. Coiling, wrapping, and twining with wool, sea grass, and other materials by Linda Watson. The pottery pieces are by Arlene Lopez. 39″ long x 10½″ wide.

1-16. When Helen Richards moistened the reeds to shape this piece, the sisal automatically unraveled. 9″ high x 5¼″ wide.

2 MATERIALS AND TOOLS FOR BASKETRY

MATERIALS

All three categories of matter — animal, vegetable, and mineral — have been used in basketry, with vegetable fibers the predominant category by far. Baskets were made to be used, so sturdy fibers were preferred by the basketmakers. Fur, feathers, bone, teeth, shells, stones, and horn were used chiefly for decoration. Some materials were suitable as they were found, but many of them had to be prepared through some simple process such as splitting, debarking, or soaking before they could be woven. Other materials needed long and involved processes to prepare them, and one wonders how many experiments failed before a suitable process evolved.

Many plants, such as grasses, vines, rushes, and ferns, have furnished suitable material for basketry. In some cases the bark of trees was used; in others their roots, fruit, or gum may have furnished the weaving fiber, dye, or waterproofing. Leaves, stems, and seeds also have usable parts.

Each geographic area has its own vegetation that has been found to be suitable. A list from a tropical area would be quite different from one prepared for a temperate zone. In fact, the materials that are available to the basketmaker determine to a great extent the kinds of baskets that are made and the techniques that are used to produce them. For instance, plaiting has developed in great variety in tropical areas where the long strands of the palm, conveniently spaced on the stem, are available, while twining and coiling are more prevalent where vines and grasses are abundant. Excellent willows are native to England and parts of Europe, so wickerwork composes much of the basketry in those areas. Splint baskets will be found where hardwoods, such as elm, ash, and oak, grow. Throughout Indonesia, Malaysia, China, and Japan, most of the baskets are made with bamboo, cane, and rattan. These versatile materials can be split into any width or thickness, so they can be used for the largest burden baskets as well as the finest and most delicate pieces.

Practically all the natural materials used for basketry in the past are still available today, if the source can be reached. The "if" is a big one though, because many craftsmen live in cities, and even in a rural area it is not always possible to gather a desirable material without trespassing. And even if the materials are obtainable, the harvesting and preparation may be time-consuming, and space is needed for drying, storing, and perhaps dyeing. There is certainly a satisfaction in gathering and creating with natural materials, but it is equally satisfying to turn to the supplies that are easily available to us today and create objects of our time with the old techniques. Let us enjoy and appreciate the skill of the basketmakers of the past and the beauty of their products rather than trying to imitate them.

In the realm of natural materials, reeds (usually of cane), raffia, sea grass, and splints can be purchased from basketry suppliers. Two sizes of reeds, a splint, and a strand of sea grass are included in figure 2-1. Cane and splints should be kept damp while they are being worked. Sometimes small whiskers or splinters are found on them after they are woven. These can be removed by singeing to give the material a smooth appearance, but care must be used, for the reeds may be discolored if too much heat is applied.

Some of the nontraditional materials that are now used for basketry are shown in figures 2-2 and 2-3. Although venturesome experimenters are making innovative designs, the same principles for selection of materials holds true for them as for any other craftwork — namely, suitability to technique and function.

plastic welting
cord in two sizes

reeds or cane in two sizes

splint

sea grass

telephone wire

jute

wire with braided cover

twisted plastic strip
from dry cleaner's bag

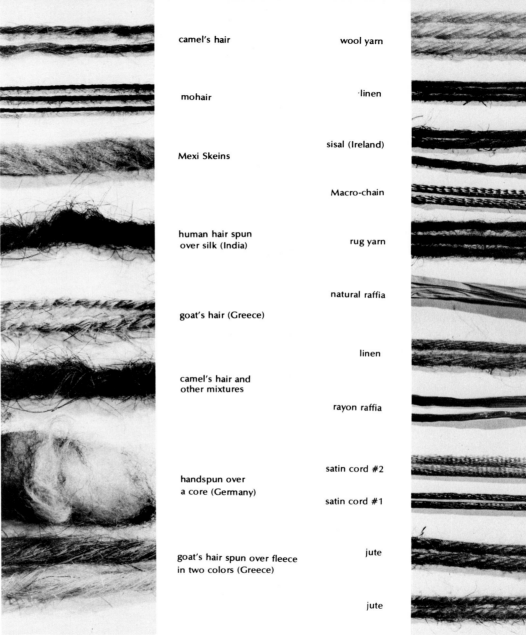

camel's hair

mohair

Mexi Skeins

human hair spun
over silk (India)

goat's hair (Greece)

camel's hair and
other mixtures

handspun over
a core (Germany)

goat's hair spun over fleece
in two colors (Greece)

wool yarn

·linen

sisal (Ireland)

Macro-chain

rug yarn

natural raffia

linen

rayon raffia

satin cord #2

satin cord #1

jute

jute

2-1. Some of the many materials that are suitable for basketry. All of them can be used for wickerwork and as foundations for coiling. The jute, the wire with a braided cover, and the twisted plastic strip might be used as wrapping material for coiling also. All but the splint could be used for twining. The splint is used in splintwork and in some types of plaiting.

2-2 and 2-3. Some materials used in contemporary basketry, primarily for coiling and twining.

2-4. A neckpiece coiled by Anita Fechter with forged copper, nickel-silver wire, and seashells. The piece is 10½" long, and the medallion is 5" in diameter.

A coiled structure that will receive wear and abrasion should be made of sturdy material. For instance, the neckpiece in figure 2-4 is made of metal and shells and shaped to fit the body comfortably. Glass fiber coiled over rope is an excellent choice for the light fixture in figure 2-5. It is resistant to heat, and since the piece will hang in space, there is little chance for abrasion, which would destroy the glass fibers. Glass fiber would be totally unsuitable for a necklace, however, because it would feel uncomfortable on the skin and also would be ruined by wear.

It is worthwhile to spend some time searching for new materials and experimenting with both old and new ones to determine the best and most interesting choices. Many hours are devoted to most basketry pieces, so a little time and judgment spent on planning is well invested if it ensures a successful conclusion.

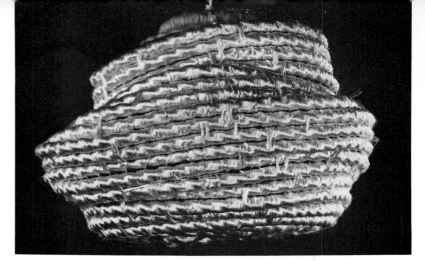

2-5. Bonnie Parker constructed this lampshade by coiling a glass-fiber yarn over rope. 15" in diameter x 9½" high.

Some materials can be used interchangeably in different techniques, but many techniques have special requirements, so further discussions of materials are included in the separate chapters.

Reeds and most other vegetable fibers can be dyed with fabric dye (such as Rit). About eight ounces of reeds can be dyed with one package, and they should be rinsed thoroughly after dyeing to remove any chemicals that may be used to process the dye.

An unchipped enamel vessel is best for the dyebath. First, the dye is dissolved in a small amount of water in a glass or other nonporous container, following the directions on the package. Then the mixture is added, with a tablespoon of salt, to warm or hot water in the enamel container. The warmer the water, the better the dye will penetrate, and the longer the material stays in the dyebath, the deeper the color will be. If an exact color is desired, it is best to test a small piece, keeping in mind that it will dry slightly lighter.

Move the reeds about in the dyebath with a stick. Leave them in the bath for about ten minutes, and check occasionally for depth of color. When the color is satisfactory, transfer the material to the rinse bath. Rinse several times, adding a little vinegar to the final rinse. Then hang to dry or place on newspapers. Additional reeds can be dyed in the same bath until the dye is exhausted.

Be sure to dye sufficient material to complete a project: it is very difficult to obtain the same color in two different batches. Dyeing is a messy process too, so it is best to dye plenty of material at one time and go through the preparation and clean-up procedures once rather than several times.

TOOLS, EQUIPMENT, AND WORK METHODS

Most basketry can be made with a minimum of tools — scissors, sturdy shears, or perhaps a knife — but there are a few pieces of equipment that will make the work easier.

For coiling, in the past, an awl was used to make the holes to lace the stitching material through. Today a sturdy needle is used, and the work progresses more easily and quickly. Scissors are needed, and sometimes a tape measure. If reed is used for the foundation, it must be kept moist, so a dampened towel or a basin of water at the worktable is useful.

For twining and wickerwork, there are some tools and equipment used by professional basketmakers that are helpful. Caneworkers use a board to hold the basket in a comfortable position. One type is placed on a table, as shown in figures 2-6 and 2-7; another rests on the floor, as illustrated in figure 2-8. If a wood base is used, a hole is drilled in the center, and the basket is fastened to the board by putting an awl (see figure 2-9) through the hole in the base and into a hole in the board. On a basket with a wicker base, the awl is inserted in the middle between the

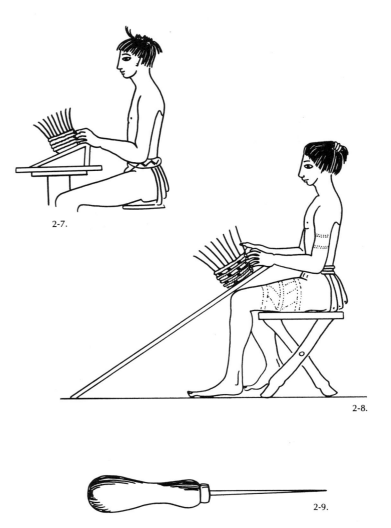

2-7.

2-8.

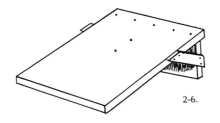

2-6.

2-9.

19

2-10. A view of the bottom of a Nantucket basket (see figures 1-12 and 5-4). This shows the ivory plug used to fill the hole in the wood base by which the basket was secured to a board for working.

2-12. Two boards held together with C-clamps were used by Vivanna Phillips to hold the reeds in place while weaving this sampler (see figure 5-1).

reeds. An ivory plug has been used to fill the hole in the Nantucket basket shown in figure 2-10. If no other method of holding a basket in place is available, sometimes a heavy object is placed in the bottom.

Pictures of Indian women working on twined baskets show that some work with the basket inverted so the bottom is upward and the basket is suspended. The spokes hang down, and the weaving progresses from top to bottom. Some twined fabrics, such as Chilkat blankets, are woven in the same manner.

Commercial basketmakers work over wooden molds to make some shapes. Crossed boards, such as the ones shown in figure 2-11, are useful to maintain a rectangular or a square shape as the basket is woven.

When a flat piece like the sampler of borders in figure 2-12 is made, two small boards and two C-clamps will hold the spokes upright so the weaving can be done.

A few other tools can be useful. Round-nosed pliers help in pulling stubborn reeds into place, and a rapping iron (see figure 2-13) is used to tap the rows of weaving to make them level. Occasionally a hammer is helpful, and a spirit lamp is convenient for singeing the hairlike splinters off finished wickerwork.

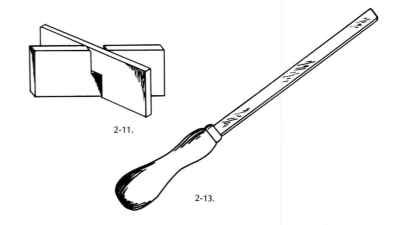

2-11.

2-13.

20

COILING 3

Coiling is the technique of stitching over a foundation and attaching rows of work together as the stitching progresses to form the basketry structure. The two elements used are the foundation, or core, and the sewing material. The foundation forms the base over which the stitching is done, and the stability of this element holds the shape of the work. Successive wraps over the foundation are made with the sewing material, which fastens back into or around one or more of the foundations or catches into the stitches of the former row to hold the work together.

Some authorities attribute the name of the technique to the spiraling form that is created when the foundation is doubled back on itself for a beginning and then wound around this beginning, row after row, as the work progresses. Others believe it refers to the wrapping of the stitching material around the core. In either case, the technique is appropriately named.

3-1. A coiled basket from Pakistan. Natural color with multicolored trimming. (Courtesy of Leslie and Fred Hart)

3-2. Lorretta Alward has created a very subtle contrast of texture by substituting a shiny material for a dull one in a few rows. (Photograph by Bonnie Schiffman)

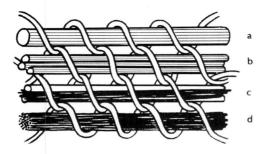

a

b

c

d

3-3. Interlocking coils on: (a) single-rod foundation.
(b) multiple-rod foundation, (c) mixed rod and grass
foundation, (d) bunch of grass for foundation.

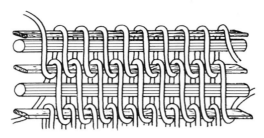

3-6. Rod and
splint (or welt)
foundation—
coiling over
three
foundations.

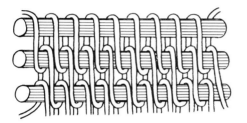

3-4. Single-rod foundation—
coiling over two foundations.

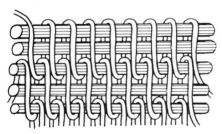

3-5. Two-rod foundation—
coiling over three foundations.

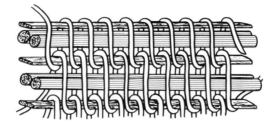

3-7. Two-rod and splint foundation—
coiling over three foundations.

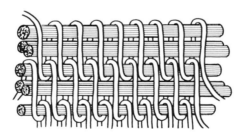

3-8. Three-rod foundation—
coiling over three foundations.

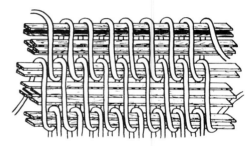

3-9. Splint foundation—
coiling over three foundations.

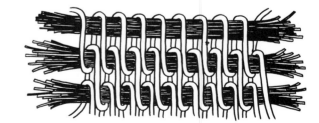

3-10. Grass foundation—
coiling over two foundations.

FOUNDATION MATERIALS

A foundation is usually some moderately flexible material available either
in a long length or in shorter lengths that will combine to form a long,
continuous strand. The strand needs to be stiff enough to hold the shape
of the article, but it must also be flexible enough to bend around a curve
or an angle without splitting or breaking. Many different kinds and combinations of materials have been used, as illustrated in figures 3-3
through 3-10.

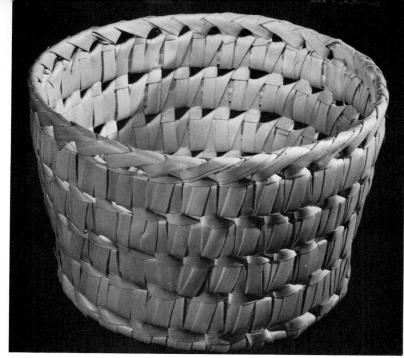

3-11. Unusual foundation and stitching materials are combined in this little basket. Place of origin is unknown. 7″ in diameter (at top).

The round strands or rods that form foundations have come from such plants as honeysuckle, willow, hazel, or cane. Reeds, available from craft-supply shops, are an excellent foundation material, but they must be kept damp during the work to retain their flexibility. Some types of cordage work well — smooth jutes or linens, or any of the various welting materials used by upholsterers, are firm, round, flexible foundations. Sea grass is another material that has found favor with contemporary craftsmen, and it is available from some yarn and basketry suppliers. A tightly twisted paper material is sold by basketry suppliers also, but some consideration should be given to the function of the piece in which it is to be used. Paper lacks the durability of some of the other foundations, particularly when it is exposed to moisture.

Wood splints and cane are less flexible than cordage and grasses, but they can be used for foundation materials on a piece with a gradual curve. To make splints, a log is split several times with an axe; then a jackknife is used to start the splint. The piece is pulled away from the wood by hand and carefully kept to uniform thickness and width. After the strips are removed from the log, they are trimmed and scraped to make them as smooth and uniform as possible.

The shiny outer surface of cane is cut from the harvested stalks and trimmed with a jackknife. Rattan is a comparable material which can be substituted for cane if cane is not available. It is sold at some upholsterer's shops or by mail order from suppliers of caning materials.

Bunches of grass are not unusual foundations for coiling, and they are a good choice if the stitching is to penetrate the foundation (as, for example, in figure 3-26). Many different grasses have been used, and authorities differ on their preparation. Some recommend that the grass should be harvested in the spring or summer, when it is green, then left to dry before using. Others suggest fall harvesting, after the grass has dried on the plant. Regardless of when the grass is harvested, it must be thoroughly dried before it is used. Shrinkage occurs in the drying process, and, unlike reed foundations, if partly dried grasses are used, a firm structure will become loose and lose its stability as the foundation materials dry out.

Interesting effects can be achieved by varying the size of the foundation over which a row of coiling is done. Uniformly wide wood splints were used for the plant container shown in figure 3-11, while various sizes of foundations were used in the basket from Ethiopia shown in figure 3-12, producing an unusual and attractive surface pattern.

3-12. An Ethiopian basket, natural with a red, green, and blue pattern (see figure 3-122). 8″ long x 6″ wide x 4″ high.

3-13. A basket and lid made by Mieke Solari with Irish sisal coiled over sea grass in the figure-eight technique. The extra color is carried along with the foundation. 11" high x 10" wide.

3-14. Detail of a coiled soft sculpture by Glada Mae Henderson.

STITCHING MATERIALS

The materials for stitching must be more pliable than those for foundations, but they must also be tough enough to stand the abrasion of the sewing and the tension created when the stitches are tightened on the foundation. Some grasses are tough enough. Various kinds of rushes have been used, as well as some split roots, such as cedar or spruce.

Raffia, which is readily available, is an excellent stitching fiber. Almost any yarn can be used, but a material without much elasticity is preferable. Rug wools, linen embroidery floss, some braided nylon seine twines, and some jutes are suitable. Irish sisal was coiled over sea grass in figure 3-13. Mixed wools, rayons, and raffias create handsome textural changes in the surface of the piece shown in figure 3-14. Rug wools were coiled over sea grass, and softly spun thick and thin wools were looped into the surface to add color and texture in figure 3-15. Irish sisal, Mexican wool, and rug wool were coiled over sea grass to make the container, and ceramic nubs ornament the surface of the piece in figure 3-16.

Many unusual materials, such as soft plastic tubing, ribbons, and strips of plastic dry-cleaner's bags or fabric, are used by craftsmen today who are searching for new effects. The choice is extensive; to find the best material for a project, try several in samples, then choose the one that gives the desired effect.

3-15. Various wool yarns were coiled by Peg Paige over sea grass to make this lidded container. 9" high x 5½" wide.

METHODS OF COILING

Basketmakers have developed many coiling techniques. Following are directions and illustrations for the more popular ones and some variations on them. In the drawings, the stitching material and the foundation coils are spaced to show the interlacement of the elements, so the drawings do not represent the appearance of the worked structure. Most of the techniques are illustrated with a photographed sample showing the finished appearance of the structure. The samples were coiled with materials that allow the interlacement to show clearly. Dixie tufting twine was used for the stitching element, and 5/32 jute (third from the bottom in figure 2-1) for the foundation, unless otherwise noted.

In contrast to the more typical spiral structure of coiling, these samples were made in rectangular shapes, which are easier to follow. The spacing of the wraps for a rectangular beginning is included with the explanation of each technique. Since there are many kinds of spiral beginnings and most of these techniques could be started in several ways, methods for beginning with a spiral are described in the latter part of this chapter.

The terms *working foundation* and *previous row* refer to specific parts of the work, and they are designated in figure 3-17.

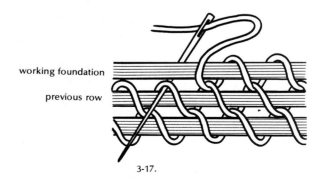

working foundation

previous row

3-17.

3-16. *A Container for My Treasures* by Helen Richards. Irish sisal, Mexican wool, and rug wool were coiled over sea grass. The ceramic nubs were made by Arlene Lopez. 16½" high x 7¾" wide.

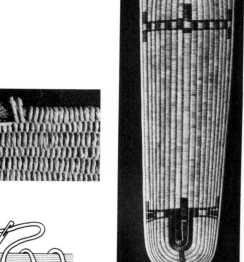

3-18.

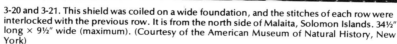

3-19.

3-20 and 3-21. This shield was coiled on a wide foundation, and the stitches of each row were interlocked with the previous row. It is from the north side of Malaita, Solomon Islands. 34½" long × 9½" wide (maximum). (Courtesy of the American Museum of Natural History, New York)

3-22.

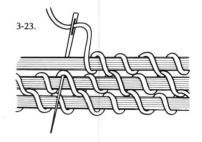

3-23.

3-24.

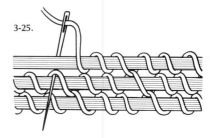

3-25.

Method I

Wrapping over the working foundation and interlocking with stitches into the previous row or rows. The foundation of the first row is wrapped, then the stitches of the second row interlock into the first row, the third into the second, etc.

Variation 1: Interlocking into each stitch of the previous row (figures 3-18 and 3-19). Imbricated coiling, which is discussed and illustrated on page 53, could be classed as an extension of this variation.

Variation 2: Alternate wraps over the working foundation are interlocked into alternate wraps of the previous row (figures 3-22 and 3-23).

Variation 3: Each third stitch is interlocked into each third stitch of the previous row (figures 3-24 and 3-25).

26

Method II

Wrapping over the working foundation and stitching into the foundation of the previous row, or into both the stitches and the foundation of the previous row.

Variation 1: Wrapping over the working foundation and stitching through the foundation of the previous row (figure 3-26).

Variation 2: Same as 1, except that the stitches interlock with the stitches of the previous row (figure 3-27).

Variation 3: Same as 1, except that the stitches pass through the back of the stitches of the previous row as well as the foundation itself (figure 3-28).

Variation 4: Same as 3, except that the stitches pass through the foundation and the front of the stitches of the previous row (figure 3-29).

Variation 5: Stitches pass through the foundation and through the front and back of the stitches of the previous row (figures 3-30 and 3-31).

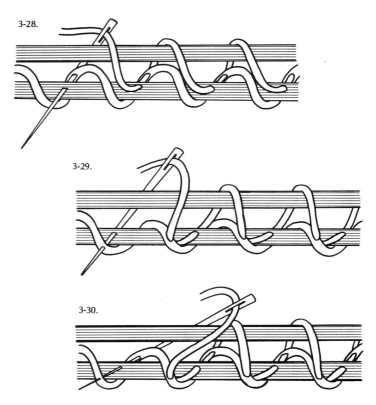

3-28.

3-29.

3-30.

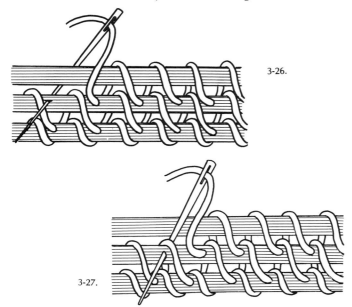

3-26.

3-27.

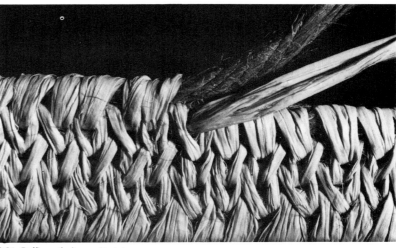

3-31. Raffia coiled over 5/32 jute.

Method III

Wrapping over the working foundation plus one or more previous rows.
Variation 1: The stitching element is wrapped over two foundation coils, and the stitches of a row alternate with the stitches of the previous row (figures 3-32 and 3-33). To begin the work, the foundation of the first row is wrapped and spaced to allow one stitch from the second row to be wrapped alternately with each stitch of the first row. (The back and the base of the chair in figure 1-2 were made with this technique.) Alternating colors of stitching material in the rows is shown in the piece in figure 3-34. Working one row from left to right and the next row in the reverse direction, and slanting each row of stitches in the opposite direction changes the surface pattern, as shown in figure 3-35.

3-34.

3-32.

3-33.

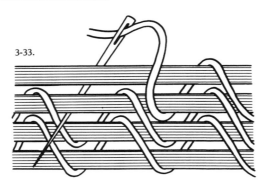

3-35. Braided nylon coiled over plastic welting cord.

28

3-38.

Variation 2: Same as 1, except that the stitches are spaced in pairs (figures 3-36 and 3-37). The stitches on the first row of the foundation are wrapped in pairs and spaced to allow room for pairs of stitches between them. Two rows of one color were alternated with two rows of another color in figure 3-38.

Variation 3: The stitching element is wrapped once over the working foundation, then over the working foundation and the foundation of the previous row. These two stitches are repeated, and the long stitches pass between the long stitches of the previous row (figures 3-39 and 3-40). The first row of this coiling technique is the same as the first row of variation 1. This stitch, or variations where several wraps are taken over the working foundation between wraps over two foundations, is sometimes called the *Lazy Squaw Stitch*, the *Peruvian Coil*, or the *Peruvian Stitch*.

3-39.

3-36.

3-37.

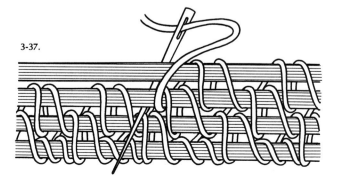

3-40.

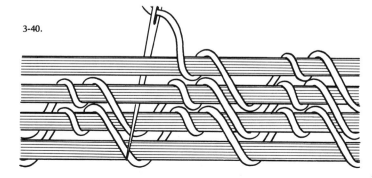

3-41. Rayon raffia coiled over plastic welting cord.

3-42.

3-43. Helen Richards made this small container by coiling rug wools over jute. 4″ high x 3⅓″ wide.

Variation 4: When two long wraps over two foundations are alternated with one wrap over the working foundation, and the work is circular, an interesting pattern of Vs can be arranged so they radiate from the center (figure 3-41). This arrangement of stitches is sometimes called the *West African Stitch*.

Variation 5: Same as 2, except that there are two wraps over the working foundation before the long stitch over the two foundations is taken (figure 3-42). The first row has two wraps, then a space for the long stitch from the next row.

Other variations with three, four, or more wraps between the long stitches over two foundations are used. In fact, the spacing can vary within one piece. Figures 3-43 through 3-46 are examples of some current work made with these techniques. The geometric patterns of triangles in figures 3-47 and 3-48 were created by contrasting wraps over a single foundation with stitches that extend over two rows of the work. A

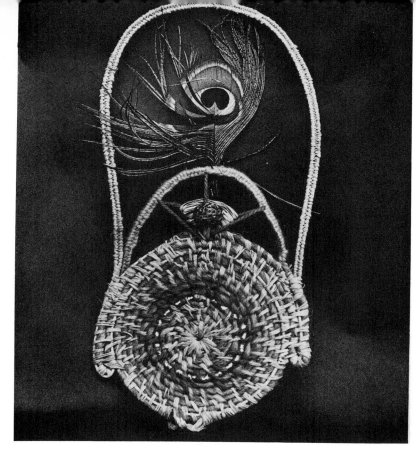

3-46. Detail of a two-colored wall hanging by Joan Michaels Paque. The technique is Lazy Squaw coiling, wrapped three times on the working foundation between the long stitches. (Photograph by Henry Paque)

3-44. A peacock feather decorates this small, coiled hanging by Bonnie Gooch. (Photograph by Bonnie Schiffman)

3-47.

3-48.

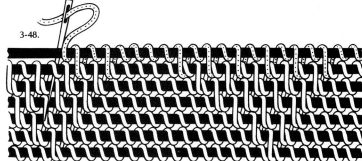

3-45. Tan, gray, and grayed purple raffia, red linen, and natural sisal are the materials in this small, sculptural piece by Jean Contreras. 4" high x 3" wide.

3-49. Rapunzel, created by Ann Meerkerk.
Tan, brown, and green Celtigale
were used for the coiling.
9¼" high x 2½" in diameter.

diagonal pattern of long stitches makes the body of Rapunzel interesting in figure 3-49. The pattern of the footed bowl in figure 3-50 has random stitches over two coils. The placement of the double stitches in the basket-shaped sculptural piece (figure 3-51) was dictated by structural need rather than the creation of a patterned arrangement. In figure 3-52, the coiled edge of the small, circular trivet holds the interlaced reeds of the center with a pattern of elongated stitches. The pattern on the shallow bowl in the background of figure 3-53 was created by varying the number of coils that the stitching element spans. The Vs in the center design were formed by angling the direction of the stitches.

3-50. A footed bowl of raffia and reeds by Joaline Stedman (see figure 7-87). (Photograph by Bonnie Schiffman)

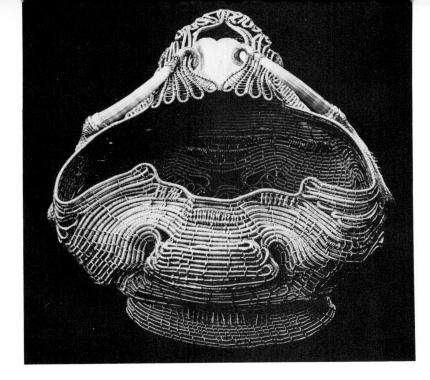

3-51. Coiled sterling-silver
wire sculpture by Anita Fechter.
(Another view of the work
shown in the frontispiece.)

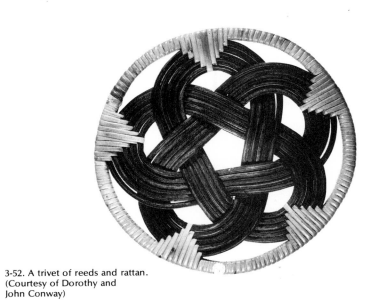

3-52. A trivet of reeds and rattan.
(Courtesy of Dorothy and
John Conway)

3-53. Nigerian wooden figures clothed in woven raffia stand before a shallow bowl (see figure
3-81). On the left is a small sweet-grass coaster. The tallest figure is 12" high. (Bowl and coaster
courtesy of Jean and Ron Wilson; figures courtesy of Leslie' and Fred Hart)

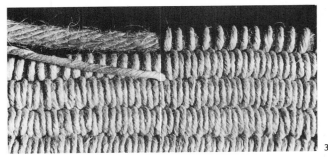

3-54.

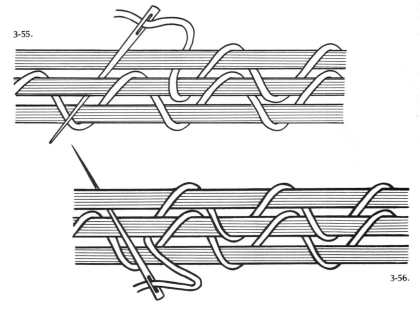

3-55.

3-56.

The direction of the wrapping for this technique can be reversed if desired, and any one of the variations shown for Method III (figure 3-57, for example) plus many other combinations can be used. Figures 3-58 and 3-59 show color and spacing variations, and figures 3-60 and 3-61 are articles made with the figure-eight technique.

3-57.

Method IV
Wrapping with stitches that form a figure eight, frequently called *Figure-Eight Coiling* and sometimes the *Navajo Stitch*. Here the stitching element passes under and behind the working foundation, continues over the top of it, comes down over the front, then passes from front to back between the working foundation and the coil used for the previous row, passes behind the lower coil, continues under the lower edge of it, comes up over the front, and finally passes between the coils, again from front to back, where it is in position to repeat the same sequence of wraps (figures 3-54, 3-55, and 3-56). To begin, the first foundation should be wrapped so that stitches from the next row will alternate with the wraps over the first foundation.

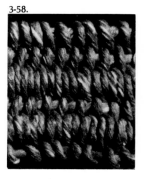

3-58.

3-59.

3-60. A three-dimensional hanging with a bell inside that sounds when it moves. It was made with a mixture of wool, jute, raffia, sisal, and other fibers in many colors by Rande Gottlieb. 6″ high x 9½″ wide.

3-61. This bright red strawberry with a green leaf, made by Marge Trout, is a free-hanging sculptural piece of rug wools coiled over jute. 20½″ high (overall); berry is 8½″ high x 6½″ wide. (Courtesy of Jean and Hugh Tillman)

Method V

In this technique, sometimes referred to as the *Lace Stitch*, the stitching element wraps first over the working foundation, then over two foundations, and finally over the stitching element itself, where it bridges the two foundations (see figure 3-64). For brevity, this long stitch and the wrap over it will be called a *horizontal cross*. In most stitching materials, the horizontal crosses create enough bulk to make it necessary to space them with at least one wrap over the working foundation between them.

Variation 1: The sequence for this variation is one wrap over the working foundation, followed by one horizontal cross (figures 3-62, 3-63, and 3-64). Working two colors in alternate rows is shown in figure 3-65. When this sequence is followed and two wraps are taken between the foundations, the stitch is known as the *Samoan Stitch*. Most of the hat in figure 3-66 was made with this stitch. Three wraps over the working foundation followed by one horizontal cross were taken in figure 3-67. Occasional rows of the lace stitch with several wraps between each horizontal cross were used to add extra pattern to the sculptural piece in figure 3-68.

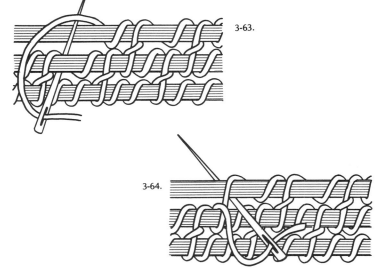

3-63.

3-64.

3-62.

3-65 and 3-66. Two small samples made by Joan Michaels Paque. (Photographs by Henry Paque)

3-67. A hat of a very fine, supple natural material similar to raffia. It is decorated with blue, white, and red cotton yarn. Attributed to Bakete, Bakuba, Lakengu. 2" high x 7" in diameter.

3-68. Rug wools were coiled over jute by Marge Trout to make this tall, sculptural container. Handwrought metal and glass beads add extra interest to the design. 16" high (with lid) x 6½" wide (maximum).

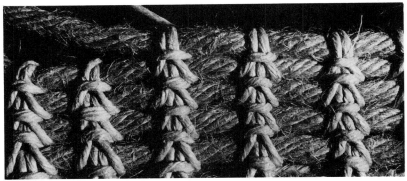

3-71.

Variation 2: Horizontal crosses are spaced with four wraps over the foundation; the long stitch for the cross is placed between the second and third wrap of the previous row (figures 3-69 and 3-70). To begin this technique, the first row of the foundation should have five wraps, then space for one stitch from the next row to be worked, and again five wraps and a space.

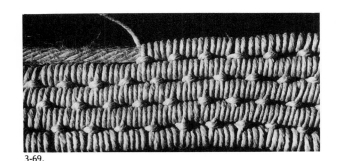

3-69.

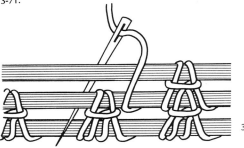

3-72.

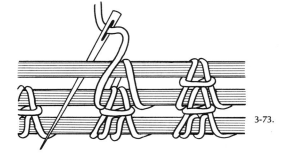

3-73.

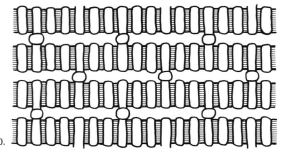

3-70.

Variation 3: In this technique, which could descriptively be named *A Stitch,* pairs of long stitches with a horizontal cross that spans both of them are placed on the foundations in vertical rows so the foundation is exposed between the rows (figures 3-71, 3-72, 3-73, and 3-74). To begin this technique, the first foundation is wrapped with pairs of stitches, spaced as desired for the vertical rows of stitches to be worked.

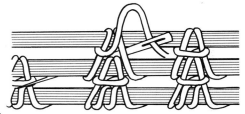

3-74.

Variation 4: This variation might be called *V Stitch*. Like the other variations, it is worked from right to left, but it differs from them in that each coil is placed below the previous one, and the work progresses downward instead of upward. The stitching element wraps over both the working foundation and the loop extending between the stitches of the previous row, first to the left of the stitch of the previous row, then to the right of it, then over the stitching element itself in a left-to-right direction at the base of the V (figures 3-75, 3-76, 3-77, and 3-78). The stitching material in figure 3-75 is white plastic lacing cord, and the foundation is ⁵/₃₂ jute.

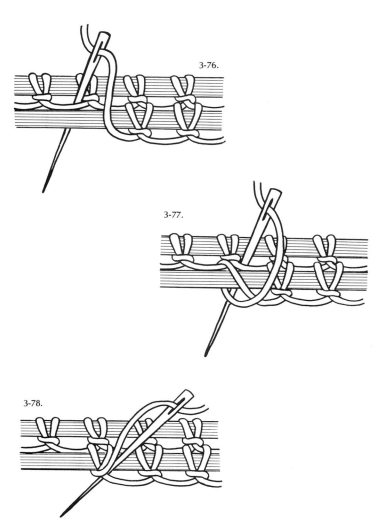

3-76.

3-77.

3-78.

3-75.

Method VI

In this technique, the stitching element wraps over a foundation, leaving space between the stitches for the stitches of the next row to loop through. Although it is usually worked in the traditional manner of coiling, it seems easier to stitch on the lower rather than the upper edge, as shown in figures 3-79 and 3-80. Each stitch wraps over the working foundation and through the spaces between loops of the previous row, with the needle progressing from front to back so that it goes behind the working foundation as well as the cord that extends between the loops of the previous row, then over itself as it comes to the front to begin the next wrap.

This interlacement has been used by the Yahagan Indians of Tierra Del Fuego, and it is usually called *Fuegian basketry.* The clothing of the strange little character on the left in figure 3-81 is made with this technique with spaced loops. A light-colored raffia is wrapped over a strand of dark raffia.

Worked without a foundation, as shown in figure 3-82, this structure has been used for many articles. In primitive cultures, many nets, bags, and other carrying devices were made with it. (It is also the basic stitch of needle lace, and in stitchery it is known as *Blanket Stitch* or *Buttonhole Stitch.*)

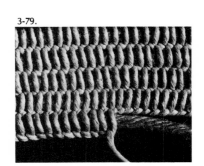

3-79.

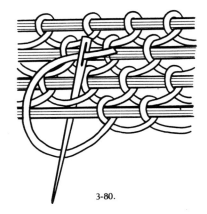

3-80.

3-81. Another view of two small African wood figures dressed in raffia (see figure 3-53). The technique used in the piece on the left is Fuegian coiling; the right-hand figure is woven or plaited.

A

B

1
2

3-83.

3-82.

3-84.

3-85.

3-86.

Method VII

This technique is a combination of coiling and plaiting. Two stitching elements are coiled over two foundations and plaited over each other between them. Figure 3-83 shows a foundation cord doubled so there are two sections to work over, A at the left and B below it. In these diagrams, two strands of different colors are used to work over the foundations so the movements of the two elements can be followed more easily. One strand can be used by looping it over the foundation cord at the fold and using the two ends for the two elements. After the cords are started at the fold, strand 1 goes under A on the right side from right to left, passes behind it, and continues over the foundation, going in front of it from right to left. Meanwhile, strand 2 enters under strand B from right to left, crosses over strand 1 between the foundations, continues in a right-to-left direction under foundation A, then goes around and over it from right to left. Next, strand 1, which has continued over (right to left), around, and under B (right to left), now crosses over strand 2 between the foundations, then continues under, around, and over A (right to left). Strand 2 continues over, around, and under B as at the beginning (see figure 3-84), and both of the strands repeat the same sequence to continue this structure.

Wrapping and interlacing the two strands together seems easier than wrapping one strand first, then working the second one into the structure; however, it can be done either way. To show the interlacement more clearly, a second foundation is added in figure 3-84. It is held in place by one strand, but two strands could be interlaced simultaneously in this row and all subsequent rows if desired. Figure 3-85 shows the second strand being woven into the structure to complete this row, and figure 3-86 shows the second row almost completed. The same system of wrapping and crossing used in the first row is repeated for each following row, with adjacent rows sharing a common foundation and the stitches fitting into each other as they pass around the common foundation.

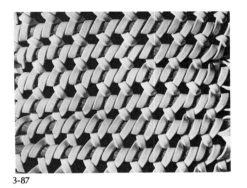

3-87

The stitching material in figure 3-87 is white plastic lacing cord, and the foundation is twisted wrapping twine. The size of the foundation cord and the size and stiffness of the working strands will determine the density of the structure, because the crossing of the two strands between the foundations hold the foundations apart, and the larger the material, the greater the distance between the foundations.

Figure 3-88 shows a small basket made with this technique, and the detail in figure 3-89 shows the structure clearly.

3-88 and 3-89. A small basket of cane and rattan. 7½" long ×5" wide × 2½" high. (Courtesy of Vivanna Phillips)

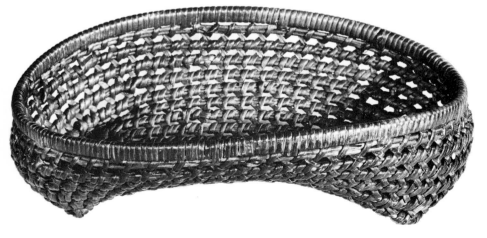

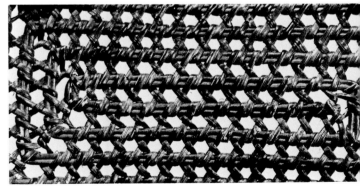

BEGINNING AND SHAPING

Basketmakers have used coiling primarily to make circular forms, and these forms are made over a foundation that spirals. The curves at the beginning are small, so the foundation material must be flexible. Before the spiral is begun, the stitching material is wrapped over the foundation a few times, spacing it to allow for the stitches of the next row. The end of the stitching material is secured and hidden as shown in figure 3-90. After several wraps, the foundation is folded back on itself in a tight circle (see figure 3-91); then the stitching material begins to wrap over the two foundations. Figures 3-92 and 3-93 show the continuation of this circular beginning. This beginning is suitable for a technique that requires wrapping over two foundation rows; if another coiling technique is used, the spacing of the stitches on the foundation may differ. For instance, if the stitches are to be interlocked into the stitches of the previous row, the foundation would spiral in the same way, but the stitches would be spaced compactly on the foundation.

Sometimes the foundation material is not flexible enough to bend into a small circle. One solution to this problem is to use a more flexible foundation for a few rows, and then substitute the other foundation. Sometimes a ring, a bead, or a circle of wood, ivory, or leather with holes for the stitches at the edge is used until the curve of the circle is not too abrupt.

After the first wraps over the foundation are made, it is always difficult to hold the work in a tight circle to make the beginning stitches. Sometimes it takes more than one attempt before a satisfactory beginning is made. Tapering the end of the foundation will help to make a neat beginning.

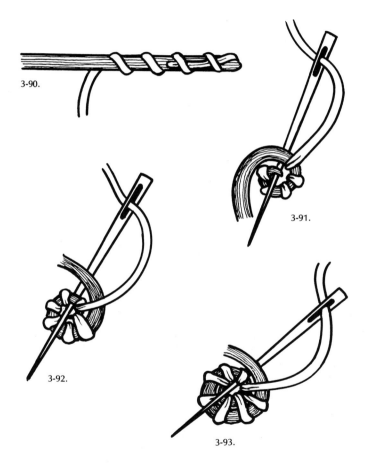

3-90.

3-91.

3-92.

3-93.

43

An oval or rectangular shape is easier to begin, because there is more to hold. If the work is to be coiled over one foundation, it is begun as in figure 3-90, except that the foundation is covered with the wrapping, because it is not necessary to leave space for succeeding rows. When the coiling is to span two foundations, the wrapping should start at the bend, as shown in figure 3-94. Figure 3-95 shows how to continue an oval form with this technique. The table mat in figure 3-96 was coiled in a rectangular form by working back and forth, then around the perimeter to complete the mat. Figure 3-97 shows this method of shaping and finishing.

3-96. The foundation of this table mat was wrapped with a tan and brown raffialike material. Split coiling stitches hold the wrapped foundations together in four places across the rows. (Courtesy of Myra R. Young)

3-94.

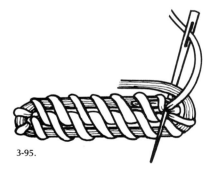

3-95.

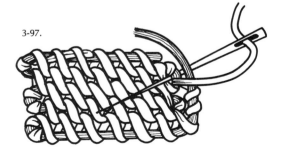

3-97.

Sometimes a knot can be used for a beginning (a square knot might be substituted for the overhand knot shown in figure 3-98). If many strands are to be used for a foundation, you can begin with a small woven section, as in figure 3-99. After the center is woven, the coiling begins, preferably at a corner of the woven section. All the strands are bent together in the same direction, and the work progresses along the row, first wrapping over one of the strands, then over two when the second joins the first, then over the accumulation of three, etc. The coiling continues around the perimeter of the center, adding a strand with each stitch until all of the center strands have been used. When the row around the center is completed, succeeding rows are added, using the bundle of strands that has accumulated in this first row as the foundation. The center can be square, rectangular, triangular, hexagonal, or any other shape, depending on what type of interlacement is used.

The technique that is usually shown for beginning Fuegian basketry (Method VI) can be adapted to other coiling methods very easily, because any form of wrapping can be used over the foundation. A circle of the foundation material is made by wrapping it around itself several

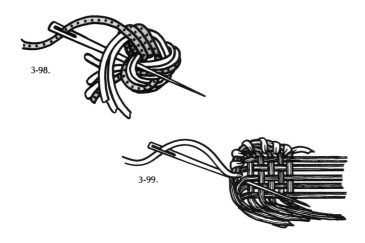

3-98.

3-99.

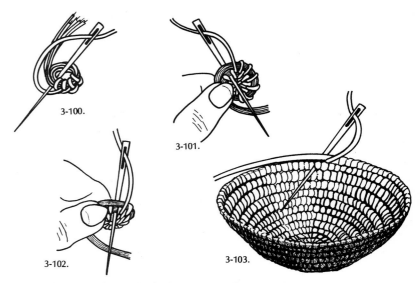

3-100.

3-101.

3-102.

3-103.

times, perhaps on the end of a finger, and then the wrapping or stitching is begun over this circle of foundation material, as shown in figure 3-100.

Similar beginnings can be used for most of the other coiling techniques and their variations, but each must be adapted to the method that is being used. The difference, mentioned previously, between coiling over a single foundation and coiling over two foundations is an example.

The position in which the foundation is held as the stitching progresses controls the shaping of the article. When the work is to be flat, the foundation is held next to the previous coil and circled around it at the point on the circumference that has the largest diameter, as shown in figure 3-101. Each row in flat circular work has many more stitches than the previous row, and they should be increased by stitching back into the same place more than once, spacing the stitches evenly.

To make a convex form, the foundation cord is held in the position that gives the desired curve to the shape as the stitching progresses (see figure 3-102). The number of stitches in a row increase as the diameter of the piece grows larger, but they do not increase so rapidly as they do in flat circular work.

The shape of the piece influences the method of work, because the best side of the work should be the side that is seen the most, and the side that faces the basketmaker is usually the best side. The inside surface of a concave piece such as a bowl is seen the most, so it should be the best side; therefore the stitching is done on the rim that is farthest away from the basketmaker, as shown in figure 3-103. Tall, slender shapes such as jars, or bulbous shapes with small openings are examples of which the outside would be the best side. They are worked on the rim closest to the basketmaker, in the manner of figure 3-102.

45

3-104. This imbricated basket made by Northwest Coast Indians has an interesting finish. (Courtesy of Warren T. Hill)

FINISHES

Most coiled baskets are considered complete when the last row of stitching is finished. To end the row, the foundation is tapered, and the stitching is continued to the end of it, so the row diminishes in size and appears to blend into the previous row, thus avoiding an abrupt ending that is unsightly. If several pieces of material are used for the foundation, they are cut off successively to taper the work toward the end. Sometimes a splint or a heavier reed is coiled on the edge to serve as a stiffening device and to increase the wearability of the basket.

The basket in figure 3-104 was finished in a particularly interesting way. The coiling was done on a spiraling foundation in the usual manner until

the third row from the top. A close look at the interior of the basket shows that the spiraling foundation tapers down to an end at the center back on the fourth row from the top. The foundations of the last three rows are not continuous but separate, like hoops, held together and to the body of the basket by the stitching element. This eliminates the tapered end on the rim of the basket. The same careful craftsmanship was used throughout the basket, making it an unusually beautiful piece.

Occasionally, a special finish is added to the rim of a coiled basket. Changes in color or in the direction of the work are some of the simplest finishes that show that special attention was given to the edge. For instance, in figure 3-105, two colors were alternated to wrap the last row, and the direction of the wrapping was reversed.

3-105.

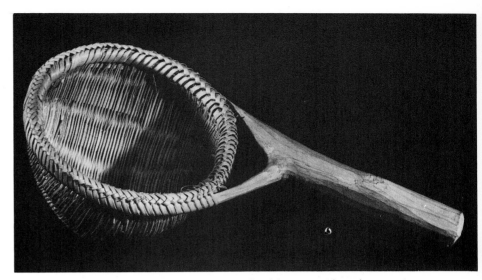

3-107. A strainer from the Laguna Province of Luzon, the Philippines. Wide spokes were shaped to fit the weave, and a forked wooden branch makes a very sturdy handle, which is held firmly by the braidlike edge. (Courtesy of the American Museum of Natural History, New York)

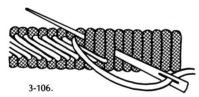

3-106.

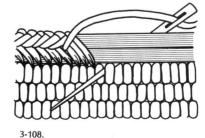

3-108.

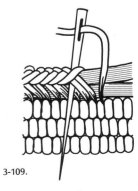

3-109.

Slanted stitches worked into the top part of the last coiled row add an attractive trim, and the stitching is more decorative if a contrasting color is used. Figure 3-106 shows the top of the last coil with a row of decorative stitching in progress. Alternate stitches can be made in different colors by using two needles, as in figure 3-105.

An edge that looks as though it were plaited (figure 3-107) can be made with the stitching shown in figures 3-108 and 3-109. The needle first passes from back to front and from right to left under a stitch of the previous row. The second movement brings it from back to front between the second and third stitches previously completed, at the same time passing between the foundations. These two steps are alternated to form a braidlike edge. If a greater slant is desired in the work, the second step can go back three, four, or more stitches. The edge can be worked over a single as well as a double foundation; in the former case the needle is inserted between the stitches and the foundation.

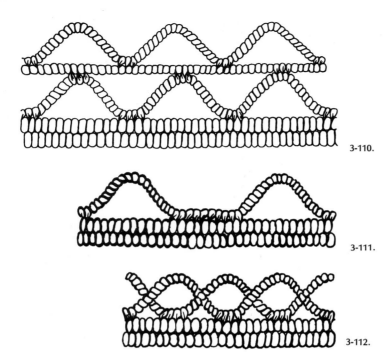

3-110.

3-111.

3-112.

3-113. Purple and tan vegetal fibers were wrapped and coiled with the figure-eight technique to fabricate this unusual basket from Rhodesia. 12″ high (with handle). (Courtesy of the American Museum of Natural History, New York)

3-114.

Starting this edge always presents some difficulty, because a previous row is required to stitch back into. Wrapping several stitches closely so they are crossed at the top of the coil will create a place where the needle can be inserted. After a few stitches, the braidlike structure on the rim begins to develop.

More elaborate edges can be used; an example is the open pattern in figure 3-110, which came from a coiled and imbricated Yakima Indian basket. The meandering line of this edge is created by wrapping and attaching the foundation alternately to the coiled rows above and below it. Many variations of this pattern are used, both as edge finishes and within the body of the basket. Sometimes one row of the pattern (see figure 3-111) is used, and at other times a piece is finished with interlocking rows, as in figure 3-112. When this design is incorporated within the basket, the contrast of density and pattern creates handsome effects. The last row of the plate from Nigeria in figure 1-11 has a similar finish, but the foundation was looped back on itself, creating a series of small, wrapped loops around the edge.

Beads, bones, shells, feathers, leather, and other found and manufactured materials can be used on the edges of baskets. Sometimes clamshell beads outline the rim of a Pomo basket. Buckskin was used as a binding for the edge by Indians of the American Northwest.

Only rarely have basketmakers departed from the traditional coiled, compact work on a spiraling foundation. The basket from Southern Rhodesia (figure 3-113) is coiled, but the wrapped sections open the structure. Similar pieces illustrated in Otis Mason's *Aboriginal Indian Basketry* are attributed to modern Peruvian and Eskimo work. Occasionally, modern baskets are coiled so that compact areas are contrasted with open sections of overlapping coils of the foundation material. A detail of this technique, sometimes called *cycloid basketry*, is shown in figure 3-114.

3-115. The coiled lid of this twined basket by Carol Shaw adds an attractive finish to the piece (see figure 7-50).

UNUSUAL EFFECTS

Modern basketmakers are creating unusual shapes by reversing the direction of the foundation in the body of the work. The handsome design in the unusual copper-wire basket (figure 3-116) was achieved by using this technique. Reversed coils make the edge of the piece in figure 3-117 the focal point of the design, and they are an important design element in the wall hanging (figure 3-118) and the winsome bird form (figure 3-119). A sparing use of several coiling techniques holds together the playful form in figure 3-120, and figure 3-121 illustrates a similar but more complex piece.

3-117. The base of this sculpture by Marge Trout was coiled with wool yarn over sea grass; the scalloped edge and lid are wool coiled over jute. 7½" high (with lid) × 5" in diameter (bottom of base).

3-118. Wrapping and coiling were combined in a small hanging by Carol A. Frisbie. (Photograph by Bonnie Schiffman)

3-119. Coiling is the predominant technique in this bird form by Richard Scott Jones. (Photograph by Bonnie Schiffman)

3-116. An unusual combination of copper wire and beads was used by Anita Fechter in this basketlike sculptural piece. 8½" long ×8" wide × 3" high.

3-120. Several coiling techniques were used sparingly to shape this abstract figure by Marta Fainberg. (Photograph by Bonnie Schiffman)

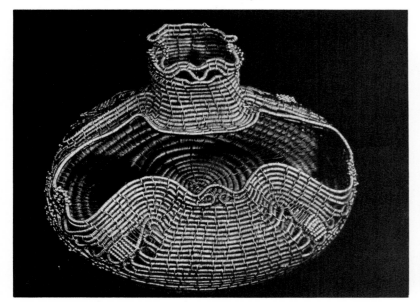

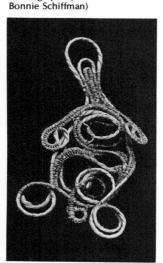

3-121. In this piece by Judy Ann Stein, dense coiling is contrasted with the more open wrapped construction around it. (Photograph by Bonnie Schiffman)

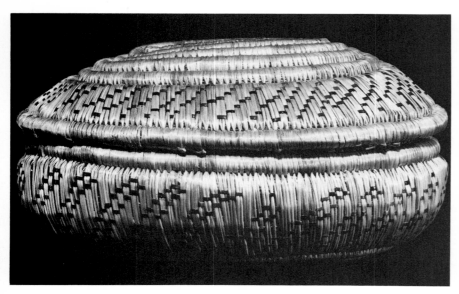

3-122. A simple pattern was introduced into the surface of the unusually wide coils of this Ethiopian basket (see figure 3-12).

3-123. The spacing of the stitches forms lines of pattern on this piece by Charlene Burningham. (Photograph by Robert Burningham)

The effects that can be obtained by changing the size of the foundation cord are discussed and illustrated at the beginning of this chapter (see figures 3-11 and 3-12). Another excellent example is the colorful Ethiopian basket shown in figure C-4 (page 99).

Pattern can be introduced on a row of coiling when it is wide enough, as illustrated in the Ethiopian basket in figure 3-122. Horizontal running stitches appear and disappear in a simple pattern over the coiled stitches. To the craftsman with an experimental turn of mind, this variation will suggest many other possibilities. The undecorated surface that is created when a wide foundation is used offers a background for design using any number of techniques.

The spacing of stitches on the foundation also can create many different textures and patterns. The flowing lines of stitches in the sculptural piece shown in figure 3-123 are an important part of the design. Spacing stitches to expose the foundation material is a design element that was used by many traditional basketmakers. Some pine-needle baskets are coiled so the light stitching material creates elaborate patterns on the brown pine-needle foundation, as in figure 3-124. Split stitches, also known as *furcated stitches,* form a part of the design on this basket, and they are frequently used on coiled baskets. Sometimes they form a line of Vs on exposed foundation coils; at other times they cover the foundation entirely, as in the basket in figure 3-125 and the detail of the stitch in figure 3-126.

3-124. Light-colored raffia was coiled over pine needles in this small basket, which was made by Mary Thorberg. 11½" long x 6" wide x 2½" high.

3-125 and 3-126. An Alaskan Eskimo grass basket. 4¾" high x 3½" wide. (Courtesy of Vivanna Phillips)

COLOR

Color changes are easily incorporated into any of the coiling techniques. Any number of strands of stitching material can be carried along the working foundation, so the color of the stitching can be changed simply by substituting one strand for another when necessary, as shown in figures 3-127 and 3-128. In figure 3-127 the end is visible. In figure 3-128 it

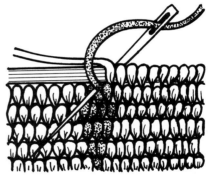

3-127.

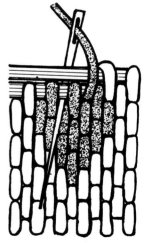

3-128.

3-129. Rug wools were coiled over sea grass by Brad Jones. The color was carried on the core and covered as the coiling was done. 10" high x 7½" wide.

Overlaying

To overlay a design in coiling, a strip of material about the same width as the foundation is carried along the working foundation. Part of the time it lies over the wrapping, and sometimes the stitches go over it as well as the working foundation (figures 3-130 and 3-131). The contrast of the stitches and the overlaid sections creates the pattern. The color of the overlaid material can be changed in a section where several of the stitches are on the surface. For instance, one color could be discontinued and a new one started under any of the groups of three stitches on the surface in figure 3-130.

is hidden behind the working foundation, where it will be covered by the stitching. If, for some reason, the alternate colors are not carried along the foundation, a new color can be introduced by placing the end of the strand on the working foundation and wrapping a few stitches over it before inserting it into the pattern.

Planning a design and placing the color changes properly is easiest when the stitches wrap over one foundation and interlock with the stitches of the previous row (as in Method I), because only one row of color is created at a time. When the stitches span two foundations, two rows are affected by each color change, so it is easy to make an error in the vertical placement of a pattern if this is not kept in mind. In comparing the diamond forms in figures 3-127 and 3-128, it is apparent that the angle of the sides is steeper in one than in the other. This characteristic should be considered when designing a pattern with any technique. Fuegian coiling and other methods that wrap over one foundation will distribute color in the same way as figure 3-127, whereas methods that span two foundations, such as figure-eight coiling and the lace stitch, will resemble figure 3-128.

OVERLAYING AND IMBRICATING

Adding a third element either by overlaying it on the foundation or by imbrication (also known as the *Klikitat technique*) is a means of producing multicolored designs.

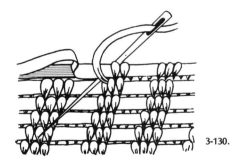

3-130.

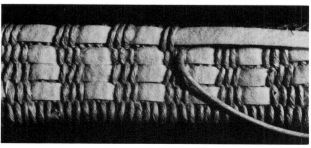

3-131.

52

3–132. The design on this Ethiopian basket was made with overlaid strands on coiling. Natural materials, in both dyed and natural colors, were used for both the stitching and the overlays. 9" high × 5½" wide. (Courtesy of Leslie and Fred Hart)

Imbricating

The word *imbricate* means "to arrange in a regular pattern with overlapping edges, as tiles or shingles on a roof." In imbricated coiling (figures 3-135 and 3-136), an extra strand of material, about the width of the coil, is carried along as the coiling progresses and is fastened with the stitches in a regular pattern with overlapping edges. To begin imbricating, the extra strand of material is fastened as in figure 3-133. Then, as each stitch is taken, the imbricating material is brought over the previous stitch, as shown in figure 3-135, and folded back so the long end of the strand is on the right and the fold extends to the left along the working foundation. The stitching material holds the folded imbricating material on the foundation by wrapping over it, then the same process is repeated by bringing the imbricating material over the stitch, folding it, and holding it in place with the next stitch. Color changes are made by substitution, as in overlaying.

The coiling techniques explained in this chapter do not exhaust all of the coiling methods used by basketmakers, but the most widely used ones have been discussed. Inventive craftsmen have developed many new variations, which the beginning basketmaker can learn about in the literature and by inspecting baskets and then explore for himself.

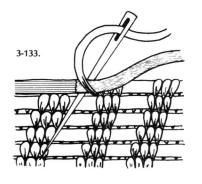

3-133.

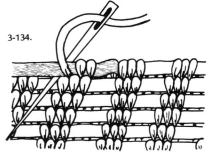

3-134.

The Ethiopian basket in figure 3-132 has an overlaid design of many colors, but the colors were changed as shown in figures 3-133 and 3-134. Instead of substituting the new color under the sections of exposed stitches, the new color is laid on the coil so the long strand extends to the right and the end of it is near where the next stitch will be placed. The strand of the former color can either be carried under the new color or clipped off after it is anchored under a stitch or two. Next, the stitch is tightened over the end of the new strand, holding the strand in place as the stitch is pulled firmly. For the pattern in figures 3-133 and 3-134, two more stitches are made on the foundation. The strand of the new color is bent back over both the stitch that holds it and the last two stitches just completed, then it is caught under the next group of three stitches, as shown in figure 3-134.

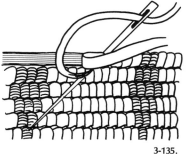

3-135.

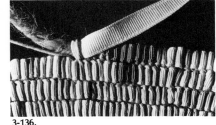

3-136.

4 TWINING

Weft twining in its simplest form is weaving two *weft* strands horizontally across a series of vertical *warps*. Each of the warp strands is enclosed by the wefts, which cross over each other or twist together between the warps. To describe the action specifically: one weft strand passes over a warp strand while the other moves under it, then the two wefts exchange positions, so the warp strand is enclosed by the two wefts. The weft that went under the last warp strand passes over the next one, and the other weft is placed in the alternate position under the warp strand. The two wefts cross again, and the twining proceeds across the row with the wefts enclosing each warp strand in turn. In most twining, the two elements (warp and weft) work at right angles to each other. Many variations of this interlacement are possible.

It is difficult to draw the line between twining that is cloth and twining that is basketry. Certainly, a Chilkat blanket would be considered a fabric. It is supple and fabric-like in hand. Twining that is stiff enough to hold its own shape usually falls in the basket category. Then where do we place the hat in figure 4-1? It is twined of wool like a Chilkat blanket, yet it is stiff enough to hold its own shape. Traditionally, hats have been made both of fabric and of basketry. What about the cornhusk bags or pouches (figures 4-2 and 4-3) that are attributed to the Nez Percé Indians? In flexibility they are about halfway between a piece of fabric and a basket. The shape of the bag is more typical of woven bags, yet the twining technique that was used is exclusive to basketry, or at least it has been in the past.

4-1. A hat twined with heavy wool. (Courtesy of Lew Gilchrist)

4-2 and 4-3. A Nez Percé cornhusk bag. Wool yarn was used for the false embroidery. 7¼" long x 5" wide.

4-4. An open form twined with raffia, linen, and wool over reed splints by Florence Okano. 6" high x 7" wide.

MATERIALS FOR TWINING

The materials used in twined basketry run the gamut from very fine, flexible yet tough grasses such as the wild beach grasses used by the Aleuts in their beautiful, small wallets to the stiff willows prevalent in England and parts of Europe. Usually the warps are round, firm materials such as reeds. Many materials can be used — hardwood or bamboo splints, some types of upholsterer's welting cords including the plastic one shown in figure 2-1, rope, clothesline, and flexible tubing. In fact, any material that has enough stability to hold its shape to twine over is worth trying. Frequently, a softer material is used for the wefts, as in figure 4-4. The choice of materials that can be used for twining is about as extensive as you care to make it. Certainly, most of the yarns and cords

(Above) 4-6. Curves held together with a little twining form a graceful sculpture by Linda Homer. (Photograph by Bonnie Schiffman)

(Below, left) 4-7. Twining over reeds, a sculpture by Nichol A. Kriz. (Photograph by Bonnie Schiffman)

(Below, right) 4-8. A sculptural piece in goat's hair, flax, and guinea feathers by Margaret Wright. The piece was started at the top and twined to the bottom, then the warp ends were pulled back through the top and wrapped to make the feathered ends emerge from the neck of the piece. 12″ high (overall) x 8″ wide.

4-5. A decorative piece combining linen, goat's hair, and feathers by Helen Richards. Coiled ridges stiffen the form, which was twined from the top down. Some of the warps were left hanging. 21″ long (overall) x 7½″ wide.

used today by textile craftsmen in weaving, knotting, and other fiber techniques make excellent wefts. In figure 4-5, many different materials were combined. Materials manufactured for other purposes, such as telephone wire, venetian-blind cord, plastic lacing, and many others are worth investigating for unusual effects.

The traditional reeds and raffia were used to form the handsome sculptural forms with flowing lines in figures 4-6 and 4-7. Figure 4-8 is a playful sculptural piece made in a more traditional basket shape. It was twined with a warp of flax and a weft of goat's hair and was decorated with guinea feathers.

Because craftsmen today are mixing techniques in new and inventive ways, the information in this chapter was chosen for its usefulness to the contemporary craftsman rather than by a strict adherence to those variations in twining that appear in traditional baskets.

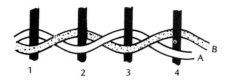

4-9.

SIMPLE TWINING

Simple twining in a left-to-right direction, as illustrated in figure 4-9, is interlaced as follows:

A is placed under warp 1, pulled forward and down, then left in that position.

B is placed over warp 1 and A and under warp 2, then warp 2 is pulled forward and down to allow space for the next passage of A under warp 3.

B is placed under warp 4, and the interlacement proceeds in the same manner.

Some variations of simple twining are shown in figure 4-10.

A simple-twined structure is made when half turns are repeated row after row. The rows can be spaced so the warps show, or they can be woven to cover the warp, forming a compact structure, as shown in figure 4-11. A surface with the diagonal pattern of a twill weave can be created by spanning pairs of warps between twists, as in figure 4-12. Here alternate pairs of warps are enclosed in the successive rows. A compact simple-twined interlacement resembles a weft-faced plain weave, and frequently the basketry technique can only be identified by the slants or twists on the wefts as they go over or between the warps.

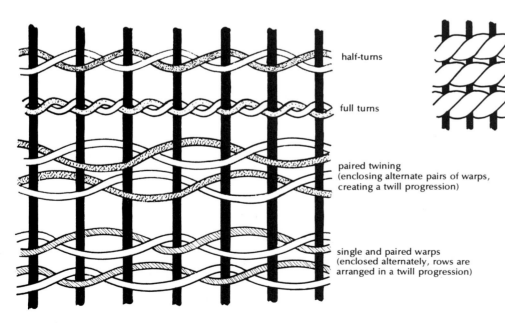

half-turns

full turns

paired twining
(enclosing alternate pairs of warps, creating a twill progression)

single and paired warps
(enclosed alternately, rows are arranged in a twill progression)

4-10. Variations of simple twining.

4-11.

4-12.

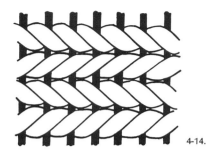

4-14.

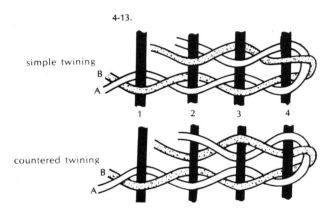

4-13.

simple twining

B
A

1 2 3 4

countered twining

B

A

4-15.

When simple twining is repeated row after row in a circular piece, the twist of each row remains the same. In a flat, rectangular piece, the wefts move back and forth across the warp, reversing at the edges. Figure 4-13 illustrates one method of reversing at the right-hand edge. The wefts are twisted in the opposite direction in the second row and subsequent alternate rows. The weaving proceeds as follows:

A is placed under warp 4 and held toward the top of the work until B is woven over warp 4 and under warp 3.

B is held toward the top of the work until A is woven over warp 3 and under warp 2, and this sequence is continued in the same manner.

If the twist of the wefts is not reversed in the alternate rows, the diagonal of each strand, as it comes over a warp, is opposite to the diagonals created in the previous row. The surface of this interlacement resembles knitting or rows of chain stitch, and it is called *countered twining* (figures 4-14 and 4-15).

58

Countered twining is not found in basketry very often, because most baskets are circular, and it is natural to continue round and round with the same twist. A detail of an Eskimo twined wallet in which countered twining was used for a border between compact and spaced twining is shown in figure 4-16. The winnowing basket from Ethiopia in figure 4-17 was twined from side to side with countered twining. The piece shown in figure 4-18 was twined continuously, and a combination of simple and countered twining was used.

4-16.

4-17. A winnowing basket of brown and tan vegetal fibers from Ethiopia. (Courtesy of Leslie and Fred Hart)

4-18. The shape of this form of Clarissa Hewitt was controlled in part by changing the size of the twining yarns. Both simple and countered twining were used to make the surface pattern (see figure 7-77). (Photograph by Bonnie Schiffman)

4-19. Plastic welting cord crossed with $^5/_{32}$ jute.

4-20 and 4-21. Plastic welting cord crossed with satin cord.

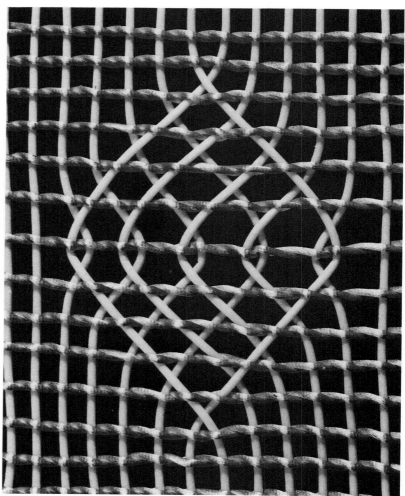

SPACING AND COLOR CONTROL

Compact twining and spaced twining create very different-looking structures, and they can be combined very effectively. The wefts in compact
twining fit together to make a thick, dense surface. In spaced twining,
warps can be crossed or manipulated in other ways to make different
kinds of open patterns, so the two structures create interesting contrasts
of density, texture, and surface pattern when used together. Figures 4-19
through 4-22 illustrate some open patterns, and figure 4-23 shows a covered bottle with spaced and compact twining combined.

60

4-22. A nineteenth-century Japanese bamboo basket with hinged cover. The technique is crossed, spaced twining. (Courtesy of the Metropolitan Museum of Art, Bequest of Edward C. Moore, 1891)

4-23. Bands of crossed, spaced twining contrast with the dense areas of compact twining in this basketry cover for a bottle. Wool was used for the false embroidery. The basketry was probably done by the Makah Indians of the Northwest United States. (Courtesy of the American Museum of Natural History, New York)

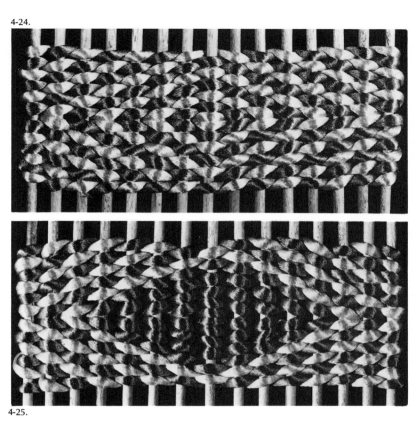

4-24.

4-25.

Patterns can be created by using strands of two colors and reversing twists. For instance, to weave the design in figure 4-24, half of the wefts in each row are twisted in one direction, and the other half in the opposite direction. After six rows are twined, the twists are reversed, so the pattern of the second part becomes the mirror image of the first. Controlling the yarns so colors alternate vertically on each warp produces the diagonal lines of the diamond.

The same directions of twists are followed for the pattern in figure 4-25, except that in the dark diamond in the center a full turn is taken each time the yarns are twisted. When a full twist instead of a half twist is taken between warps, even though two weft colors are used, the same color comes to the surface over adjacent warps.

SURFACE DESIGN ON A TWINED STRUCTURE

There are various methods of producing pattern on a twined structure by introducing additional strands that are not part of the basic structure. Such strands can be overlaid vertically and caught into the surface occasionally, a technique that Mason calls *beading*. Sometimes strands are carried over the surface in a weft direction and caught into the surface between each twist or between alternate twists: this is called *false embroidery* or *overlaid twining*. An entirely different method of color control in which two strands of different colors are woven as one is also called *overlay* in some references, thus causing some confusion of terms. A better name for the latter technique would be *twining with doubled strands*. Wrapping an extra strand over both wefts between the warps is referred to as *frapped twining*.

Varying the spacing between the twists of the twining yarns by spanning two, three, or more warps is another manipulation that gives pattern and color control. The pattern of diamonds in figure 4-26 is created in this way, with two colors.

Using two contrasting yarns makes it possible to create many patterns and textures. The contrast can be in color, texture, or both. Figure 4-27 shows seven small sections of patterns of simple twining; any one of them could be used as an allover repeat pattern or as a border design. The same is true of the patterns of countered twining shown in figure 4-28.

The artist combined macramé with twining to make the dramatic hanging shown in figures 4-29 and 4-30. The knotting elements in the half hitch became the foundation elements, or warps, for twining: for instance, the section of radiating lines was created by twining one dark and one light weft across the knotting cords. Macramé can also be useful for shaping a twined form. A row of half hitches provides an ideal opportunity to add or subtract warp strands and thus to increase or decrease the size of the piece.

4-26.

(Right) 4-27. Many patterns can be created with the simple-twined structure by using weft yarns in two colors. Cotton rug yarn was used in this sampler. (From the Shuttle Craft Guild monograph, *Weft Twining*)

(Opposite, left) 4-28. Two colors of cotton rug yarn were interlaced across each row with countered twining. The colors were controlled to create several patterns. (From the Shuttle Craft Guild monograph, *Weft Twining*)

4-29 and 4-30. *Nazar* by Joan Sterrenburg. Sculpture made of horsehair and Polytwine with twining and half hitches. 8½" long.

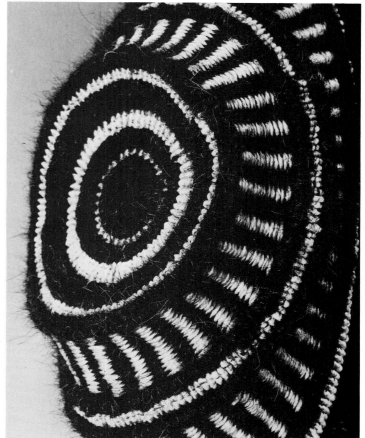

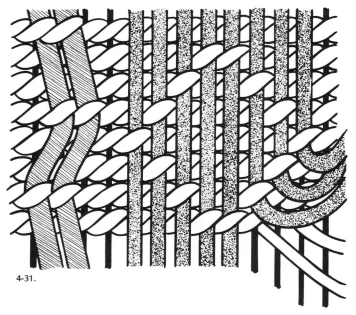

4-31.

4-32. Twining with cotton rug yarn. (From the Shuttle Craft Guild monograph, *Weft Twining*)

False Embroidery or Overlaid Twining

The Tlingit Indians had a good name for this technique — *uh tah yark tu twage*, which means, "outside lifted up and put around." This describes exactly what happens. Between twists of the two twining elements, a third strand is wrapped around the one that comes to the surface. The extra strand does not show on the reverse side of the work, because it is looped around the surface strands only. Most references show this extra strand crossing the twining strand, as shown by C in figure 4-33. It is looped under strand A, then pulled up and left until A is twined under the next warp. The second line of twining in figure 4-33 shows the next step: strand C is brought under the second twining strand B, then pulled up and left while B is twined under the next warp.

Although it seems to be the exception, the extra yarns in the cornhusk bag in figure 4-2 parallel the twining strands, as shown in figure 4-34, rather than crossing them. The extra yarn C is looped under A before it is twined under the warp, then C is looped over B before it is twined under the next warp.

Occasionally, the extra yarns are caught into the twining strand on the surface of alternate warps instead of catching into each strand as illustrated. This variation can either be used alone or combined with the previous technique, thus increasing the opportunity for surface pattern, texture, or both.

Beading

Strips of flat material can be carried over the surface of the work in a warp direction and fastened into the surface at intervals to create a pattern (for example, the diamond in figure 4-31). These extra strands do not have to remain parallel to the warp, as illustrated by the two vertical strips on the left side of figure 4-31. Figure 4-32 shows one of the many patterns that are possible with surface strands that have been diverted from vertical positions.

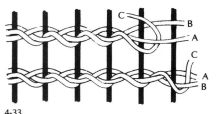

4-33.

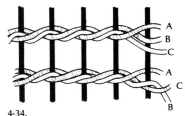

4-34.

64

4-35.

4-36.

4-39.

4-40.

Twining with Doubled Strands

In place of the two strands that weave across a row in simple twining, two pairs of strands are used, and each pair includes strands of two colors, as shown in figure 4-35. When the pattern requires a color change, the position of the two colors is reversed, as shown in the right side of this illustration. The doubled strands can be manipulated so the dark color shows on the face and the light on the reverse, as in figure 4-35, or they can be twisted so both sides show only the dark material, as in figure 4-36.

Frapped Twining

Here, an extra strand is wrapped over both twining strands at the place where they twist between the warps, producing an oblique angle on the face of the work. On the reverse side the technique will form vertical lines (figure 4-37). Examples of both overlaid and frapped twining are shown in figure 4-38.

4-37.

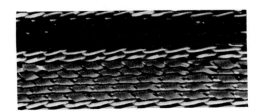

4-38. Three rows of overlaid twining and five rows of frapped twining on a ground of twined plastic welting cord. Plastic package strapping was used for the overlay; the strips of frapping material were cut from plastic shelf paper.

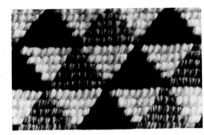

4-41. Twining with cotton rug yarn in white, turquoise, and brown. (From the Shuttle Craft Guild monograph, *Weft Twining*)

Wrapped or Taaniko Twining

Two wefts combine across a series of warps in wrapped or Taaniko twining also, and the structure of the interlacement is the same as twining with full turns. It is considered a separate technique because the appearance of the work is quite different. Basketmakers have called it *wrapped twined weaving*. For a surface of one color, it requires one relatively rigid weft and a second weft that is more supple. The rigid weft is placed behind the warps, and the second weft wraps over it and the warps, as shown in figure 4-39. The rigid weft is usually kept on the inside of the basket, and the rows of wrapping show on the outside. Sometimes the rows of twining are spaced apart, and sometimes the work is compact.

The Maoris of New Zealand use this twining interlacement (which they call Taaniko) to weave their clothing. When a fabric is woven with the technique, the weft that is held behind the work is not a rigid material, but it is held taut so the wrapping weft interlaces in the same way as it does in basketry, and only the wrapping weft shows on the surface of the fabric. Colorful patterns are woven by the Maoris in this way. Strands of several colors are carried in the position of the rigid weft. One of the wefts is used for wrapping over the warps and the other wefts, and then, according to the color that is needed to produce the desired pattern, the position of two of the wefts is exchanged, as illustrated in figure 4-40. Figure 4-41 shows a pattern of triangles woven in three colors with the Taaniko technique.

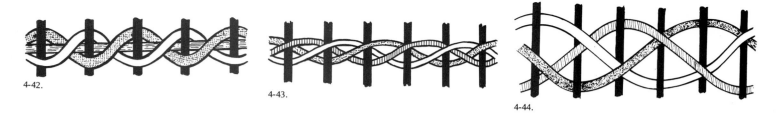

4-42.

4-43.

4-44.

Ti, Tee, or Lattice Twining

This basketry technique also has one relatively rigid weft, but it differs from wrapped twining in that it has *two* supple wefts. These two wefts are twined over the warps and the rigid weft by the simple-twining method, and each stitch encloses the intersection where a warp crosses the rigid weft (figure 4-42). Baskets woven in this way are very firm and strong. The technique is called lattice twining because the rigid wefts crossing the warps resemble latticework. Ti or tee is the Pomo Indian name for this technique, and Pomo baskets woven entirely with it are called Ti baskets.

Three-Strand Twining and Braiding

Three-strand twining gives a ropelike appearance on the surface. Each weft strand spans two warps (figure 4-43), but on the reverse side the weave resembles two-strand twining, because each strand passes under only one warp. Like two-strand twining, this technique can be woven in either simple or countered twining, or with either spaced or compact rows.

Many patterns can be created if color is used in three-strand twining, because three different colors can be woven simultaneously, and patterns can be developed by arranging the colors in relation to the adjacent rows. Additional surface variations can be obtained by adding false embroidery or frapped twining to a three-strand twined structure.

Three strands can also be braided (see figure 4-44) across a warp, and the surface takes on quite a different appearance. Again, many color combinations and patterns are possible, because three different colors can be braided simultaneously. (Technically speaking, more than three strands could be used, but I have found no mention of basketry made with more than three strands braided across a warp. Perhaps this is another area for experimental work.)

Different surface patterns can be created with braiding, depending upon how the rows are arranged. In the upper part of figure 4-45, the rows are fitted together like simple twining, while in the lower part, the weave appears more like countered twining. In the pendant in figure 4-46, the braiding resembles twining, because the soft weft material allows the rows to overlap.

4-45. Twining with plastic welting cord.

4-46. The center of this pendant by the author is a checkerwork of red leather strips. Around it linen yarns in red, orange, and brass colors were braided on the leather strands. Shiny brass beads provide contrast to the soft, dull materials.

WICKERWORK AND SPLINTWORK 5

Basket categories are not consistent. Coiled and twined baskets are grouped according to technique, but wickerwork and splintwork are classed by the material of which the baskets are made. Wickerwork refers to baskets made of any of the various reeds; splintwork, to baskets woven of splints. Plain weave and twill weave are common to both categories, but twining is used only in wickerwork, because splints are too rigid to make the twists required for twining. Some of the beginnings, edge finishes, and handles explained in Chapter 7 are also common to both categories.

WICKERWORK

Wicker furniture is probably the first thing that comes to mind when the term *wickerwork* is used. Certainly, it has a long tradition. Chairs, clothes hampers, market baskets, picnic baskets, and many other functional pieces of wickerwork are still available and popular today. Until now, this technique was used primarily for utilitarian articles, but wickerwork, along with the other forms of basketry, has a great potential for decorative sculptural pieces.

Many terms have been used for what will be considered as wickerwork here. Canework and willow basketry are forms of wickerwork. Osier basketry is synonymous with willowwork. Checkerwork and the basic weave of splint basketry have the same structure as the plain weave used in most wickerwork. Twining with cane and reed is found as frequently as the plain weave in baskets classed as wickerwork. In wickerwork, three-strand twining is called *waling,* except when it is used at the point where the warps are bent from the bottom to form the sides of a basket. Then it is called *three-rod upsetting. Four-rod upsetting,* twined with four strands, is also used in wickerwork. Very little attempt has been made in the literature on basketry to standardize terminology. Wickerwork was chosen as a general term here because it is the most inclusive and the most frequently used.

Wickerwork is made by weaving long, flexible *strands* (sometimes called wefts) horizontally over relatively inflexible, vertical *spokes* or stakes (sometimes called *warps*), which shape the piece. The strands are usually reeds of cane, willow, honeysuckle, or other slender plants. Rattan and sea grass are also used. The spokes are generally of cane or some kind of wood splint (such as oak). Plain weave, twill weave, or twining forms the structure of most wickerwork.

Many of the reeds should be kept damp for flexibility during the weaving. When the work is completed, they should be allowed to dry thoroughly, or they may become discolored from continued dampness.

four-strand twining

two-strand twining

fitching

three-strand twining
full-twist twining

circular openwork progression

splintwork

three-strand countered twining

twining—two colors

three-strand twining

doubled strands—one strand
each color, plain weave

four-strand twining
two colors paired in countered
twining

three-strand twining

plain weave—two colors

three-strand twining
countered twining—two colors,
doubled strands

three-strand twining

two-strand twining—two colors
countered twining
fitching
countered twining

plain weave—splint and reed

two- and three-strand twining

plain weave

three-strand countered twining

5-1. A sampler of various patterns
and color combinations of
wickerwork by Vivanna Phillips
(see figure 2-12).

Plain weave, or *randing* as it is called by caneworkers, is the simple under-one-over-one weave shown in figure 5-2. *Twill weave* can be a succession of under-one-over-two interlacements, as shown in figure 5-3, or one of several other combinations such as under-one-over-three, under-one-over-four, under-two-over-three, etc. Since the spokes are usually spaced apart in relation to the strands in wickerwork, the under-one-over-two weave spans the shortest distance, and it is used most frequently. Twined weaves have been explained in the previous chapter, and the structures are no different when applied to wickerwork.

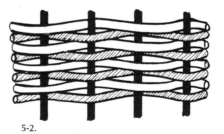

5-2.

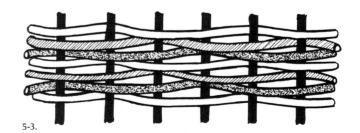

5-3.

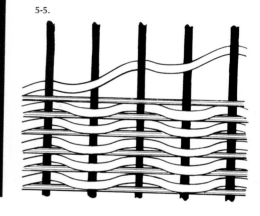

5-5.

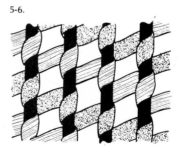

5-6.

5-4. These Nantucket baskets would be classed as wickerwork in the randing technique (see figures 1-12 and 2-10). The largest basket is 8″ in diameter x 6″ high; the smallest is 3¼″ in diameter x 3½″ high.

Usually wickerwork is woven compactly, like the Nantucket baskets in figure 5-4. Special effects can be created by varying the tension placed on the strands as they are woven. In figure 5-5 the darker strands are pulled taut, while the white ones are more relaxed.

Sometimes pattern is achieved by contrasting a twined or braided band with an area of plain weave. Simple and countered twining (or *pairing* and *chain pairing* in the language of the caneworker) are used frequently to make borders. Sometimes bands of color are introduced with dyed reeds. A sampler of wickerwork borders made with some of these different techniques is shown in figure 5-1.

An open weave with a diagonal line can be made by wrapping the spokes with a flat, flexible material. In figure 5-6, the wrapping is done with two alternating colors. In basketry, this wrapping technique is usually combined with plain weave or twining, because it does not provide a very stable structure by itself.

The number of weaves used in wickerwork are few, but many variations of pattern and texture are possible even with only one color. With more than one color, the design possibilities are extensive. Borders, handles, and other details also play an important part in the design of wickerwork basketry. These details are discussed in Chapter 7.

5-7.

SPLINTWORK

Splintwork usually refers to baskets made of wide splints. When vertical spokes and horizontal strands of equal size and number are woven into a square pattern, the interlacement is called *checkerwork* (see figure 5-7). To a weaver, this is a *balanced plain weave.* In basketry, the term checkerwork is also applied more inclusively to plaiting and other interlacements using flat, wide strands.

Splints are frequently dyed, and baskets with colorful patterns are common. The splintwork designs shown in figures 5-8 and 5-9 are adapted from Cherokee baskets.

A variation of splintwork that is seen in oriental basketry employs short lengths of splints that are inserted into the structure in various ways. Figure 5-11 is a view of the interior of the basket in figure 5-10, showing the short ends on the inside. The background appears to be a plain weave, narrow splints alternating with wide ones in the weft, and the short lengths making the herringbone pattern were inserted after the background was completed. The two baskets in figures 5-12 and 5-13 were apparently made by the same technique.

Splints may be curled as illustrated in figure 5-14 to give dimension to the surface of splintwork. Attractive patterns can be developed with this technique: in the hexagonal weave of Malaysia and the Orient (see Chapter 6), the splints are twisted to form three-dimensional parallelograms, as shown in figure 5-15. These are known as "rice grains."

5-10 and 5-11. A dark brown basket of wide and narrow splints, probably of Japanese origin. 6¾" high × 5½" wide. (Courtesy of Vivanna Phillips)

5-8.   5-9.

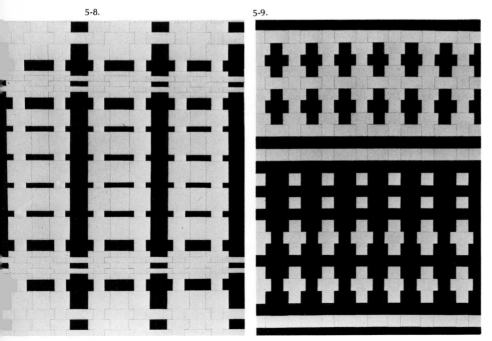

5-12 and 5-13. Nineteenth-century Japanese baskets. (Courtesy of the Metropolitan Museum of Art, New York, Bequest of Edward C. Moore, 1891)

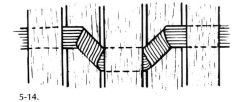

5-14.

5-15. Detail of a Mad Weave basket from Luzon, the Philippines (see figures 6-71 and 6-72).

6

PLAITING

Plaiting is a general term that is used in basketry for the interlacements of plain weave, twill weave, and some patterned weaves that are usually woven with flat strands of equal width.

TWO-ELEMENT PLAITING

Checkerwork

Checkerwork (figure 6-1), a balanced plain weave which was also mentioned in the discussion of splintwork, is the basic structure of plaiting. The basket from Mali (figure 6-2, center) is an example of a traditional use of checkerwork, and figures 6-3 and 6-4 show a contemporary application of the plain-weave structure.

6-1.

6-2. A plaited basket from Mali is the background for a small coiled container with a lid from northern Kenya and a wooden butter bottle from Ethiopia (see figures 1-11 and 7-103). The plaited basket is 14" in diameter. (Courtesy of Leslie and Fred Hart)

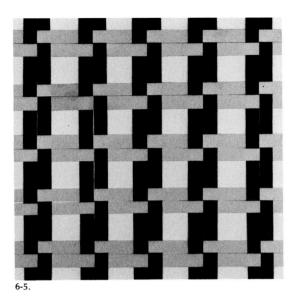

6-5.

6-3 and 6-4. Plaited newspaper constructions by Ed Rossbach. Left and detail, *An Irrelevant Solution*. 11" long x 12" wide x 12" high. Right, *Soft Construction*. 24" long x 20" wide x 17" high. (Photograph by Bob Hanson)

Checkerwork can be spaced, as illustrated in figure 6-5. One of the most functional applications of this technique is for basketry sieves. Usually the sieve is a square tray of a firm weave, with the center section of the bottom woven in open checkerwork.

Figure 6-6 is a diagram of an interlacement found on a pair of women's open-weave summer shoes. The strands are crossed between the interlacements, forming an attractive variation of open checkerwork. It should be noted that a material more supple than cane or splints, such as leather, is necessary to make the twists for this weave.

6-6.

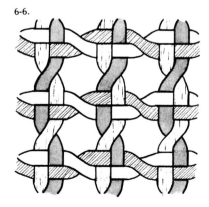

73

6-7.

6-8.

6-9 and 6-10. Basketry patterns from Philippine baskets.

Color can be added simply by overlaying strands on the original strips and weaving them in where the color is to appear, as in figure 6-7. Geometric motifs are most easily executed this way. Another effect is demonstrated in figure 6-8: narrow strands are overlaid and caught into the surface at intervals. In figure 6-9, narrow strands overlaid on wider strands produce a handsome plain-weave pattern. Extra strands added into this weave result in a pinwheel pattern (figures 6-10 and 6-11). This variation and other overlays on basic weaves are frequently found in Oriental and Malaysian basketwork, where a narrow black strand is often woven over a basic pattern of natural-colored material.

Interlacing the strands at an oblique angle makes a pattern of diamonds (figure 6-12), and variations on this weave can be produced by the same methods just discussed for the more conventional checker-work.

6-11. A small basket made of construction paper by Ann Meerkerk.

6-12.

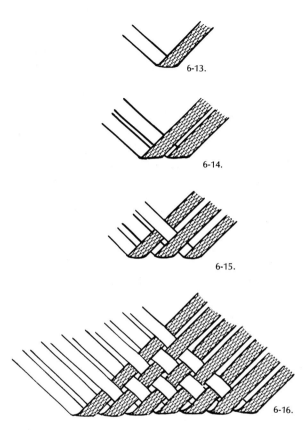

6-13.

6-14.

6-15.

6-16.

There are some methods of shaping and finishing plaited basketry that are exclusive to checkerwork, or at least seem to be used only on mats and other pieces made with a balanced plain weave.

To begin a piece with a finished edge, fold each of the strands to be used into a right angle (figure 6-13). (In figures 6-13 through 6-16, the strands are shaded on one side and light on the reverse to make the structure more apparent. For clarity, too, the strands are spaced apart, but they fit firmly against each other in the actual weaving.) The second strand is placed over the left side of the first strand (figure 6-14). The third strand is placed over the left side of the second strand and under the left side of the first strand (figure 6-15). Additional strands are added and interwoven in the checkerboard structure (figure 6-16).

75

Turning a corner to the left is accomplished by folding the left-hand end of the corner strand back so it parallels the right-hand end (figure 6-17). Subsequent strands are similarly turned at a right angle at the edge, and they continue on in the work paralleling the right-hand strands of the completed weaving. Turning a corner to the right is done in the same way, but in the reverse direction.

The top of a woven piece can be finished in a like manner. Turn figure 6-17 a quarter-turn clockwise to see the path the strands will take. As they turn back down over the woven section, they are inserted back into the structure, thus doubling the strands for a short distance, and then they are trimmed so the ends are hidden (figure 6-18).

A more decorative edge can be woven by spanning two rows of weaving at the turns with strands from alternate rows (figure 6-19).

A double surface — one layer on the top of the other, each independent of the other (except at the edges) — can be created with plaiting, as illustrated in the sequence of figures 6-20 through 6-26.

The plaiting is started with four strands, the end of each strand numbered (figure 6-20). Strand 2 is pulled back to get it out of the way temporarily.

Strand 4 is bent forward over strands 5-6 and 7-8 (figure 6-21).

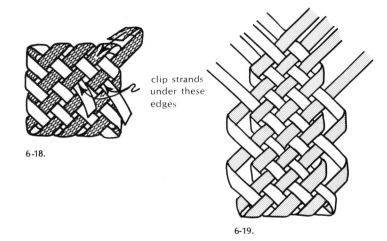

6-18.

clip strands under these edges

6-19.

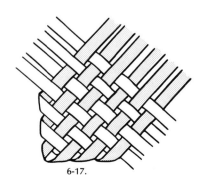

6-17.

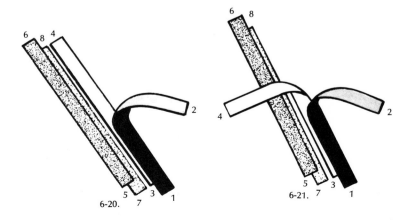

6-20.

6-21.

76

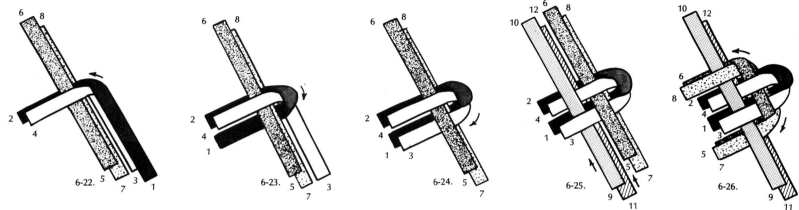

6-22. 6-23. 6-24. 6-25. 6-26.

Strand 2 is bent over strand 4 and between strands 5-6 and 7-8, remaining parallel to 4 (figure 6-22).

Strand 1 is folded and brought down under strand 7-8 so it is parallel to and on the right side of strands 2 and 4 (figure 6-23).

Strand 3 is folded over and brought down parallel to strand 1 between strands 5-6 and 7-8 (figure 6-24).

Now two more strands are added parallel to strands 5-6 and 7-8, and they are interwoven into strands 1, 2, 3, and 4. Strand 12 is woven under 1 and over 2. Strand 10 is woven under 3 and over 4 (figure 6-25). This is where the two separate surfaces first become apparent.

Strand 8 is bent forward over strand 9-10, then strand 6 is bent over strand 8 and down between strands 9-10 and 11-12. Strand 5 is bent back and under strand 11-12. Strand 7 is bent forward over strand 5 and between strands 9-10 and 11-12 (figure 6-26).

The sequence shown in figures 6-25 and 6-26 is continued until the piece reaches the desired size. The edge that is created on the left side can be duplicated on the right, as shown in the cutaway detail in figure 6-27. The dotted line represents the line of the edge when completed, where each pair of strands is bent to reverse its direction. When the desired width of the piece is woven, the strands are turned at the right edge, and no new strands are added. The strands that are folded back on the right side weave across the two surfaces to continue the piece.

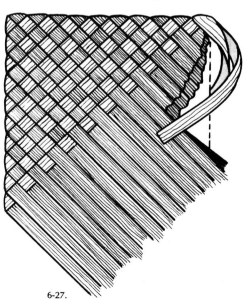

6-27.

6-28.

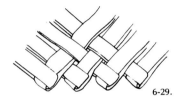

6-29.

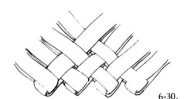

6-30.

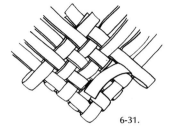

6-31.

A serrated edge is started by doubling the strands to be woven. The end of doubled strand 1 is placed between the folds of strand 2, as in figure 6-28. The two strands are fitted together so the folded edges form a 90-degree angle. Pairs of strands are fitted together in this way; then they are laid beside each other and interwoven as in figures 6-14 through 6-16. The strands can be woven double to create a single structure (figure 6-29), or the two ends of the strands can be separated and double-woven (figure 6-30), as described in figures 6-26 and 6-27.

Doubled strands can also be combined to make a straight edge, again in either a double or a single structure. The first two strands are combined as shown in figure 6-28. On the edge going to the left, the next strand is caught over the underneath part of strand 2; the following strand goes over the top part, and subsequent strands are alternated in like manner. The same system is used for the strands on the left edge. After they are inserted at the edge, they can be woven as a single structure, as shown in figure 6-31, or as a double structure.

The serrated and straight-edge methods just described can be used together to make a larger-scaled serrated edge as well. Figure 6-32 shows several points woven with straight-edge corners, and then combined into a serrated edge by weaving strands from each point across strands from the other points.

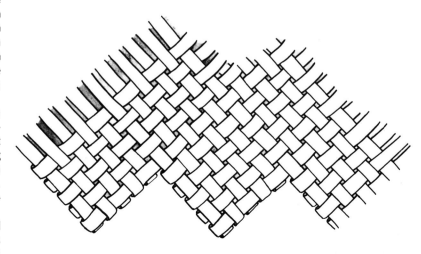

6-32.

Braids

Baskets, mats, hats, and other functional and decorative objects can be made by stitching together long strands of braided material. Braids can be made with three or more strands. Most of them have a plain-weave structure, with the strands reversing direction at the edges, but occasionally a twill weave is found in a multiple-strand braid. The structure in figure 6-19 is the same as a multiple-strand braid, but the direction of working may seem awkward, because most braiding is woven toward the worker, and the strands are generally bent forward (at least in a three-strand braid, which is the most frequently used). Figure 6-33 is more easily recognizable as a braid.

Braids are usually stitched together with a strong thread, and the sewing is done invisibly by passing the thread under alternate loops of two braids, as shown in figure 6-34. There are other more decorative methods of attaching them: an example is given in figure 6-35. An extra strand of material is couched down with the same stitching that connects the braids, thus holding them together and adding a decorative cord between them at the same time.

Another method of attaching braids requires no stitching: the strands of each braid are looped through the previous braid as the braiding progresses. This makes a thicker, sturdier weave with quite a different appearance.

The first braid is woven as usual. Then, as illustrated in figure 6-36, the second braid, which has been placed on the right, is looped back into the first one as it is braided. Each time a strand of the second braid reaches the left side, it is looped through the right side of the first braid.

To increase the size of the work, when working around a corner or a curve, for example, two loops of the second braid are caught into one loop of the first one. Skip a loop to decrease the size. A second braid can be connected to the previous one on either the right or left side when the work begins, or at any time, and this method of attaching braids can be used for braids of three, four, or more strands.

Some variations on this technique will change the surface appearance of the work. Figure 6-36 shows the attaching strand going *underneath* the loop of the first braid. Instead, it might be taken *over* the loop. Or it could reach back into the center of the first braid if a thicker texture is needed. Further variations on this technique offer the curious craftsman a good area for experimentation.

6-33.

6-34.

6-35.

6-36.

6-37.

6-38.

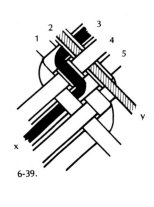

6-39.

6-40.

Some interesting braids that have been used include the edge detail shown in figures 6-37 and 6-38, which is based on a hat braid from the Society Islands. As each strand reaches the outside edge, it is turned once before it enters the work again, thus creating a small protrusion where the turn occurs. Only a material with some stiffness will hold this form. Figure 6-37 shows a turn toward the back on the left side and a turn toward the front on the right side, both in progress. Figure 6-38 shows them completed.

In other hat braids the strands interrupt their path in the pattern to make unusual edges. Sometimes two and occasionally three strands are folded back and interwoven over each other at the edge before continuing in the braid. This is another interesting area for experimental work.

Another variation that is indigenous to the Society Islands uses overlaid strands. In figure 6-39, strands X and Y are worked into the surface of a five-strand braid. To start, strand X is laid over strand 3, which goes to the left, and strand Y is superimposed on strand 2, which moves toward the right. Strand X follows strand 3 to the left under strands 2 and Y, then folds forward to the right so it lies on top of strands 1 and 4. It folds backward at a right angle and follows strand 5 as it passes under strand 3.

Next, strand Y follows strand 2 to the right under strand 4, then it is bent forward at a right angle (see figure 6-40) and proceeds left on top of strand 5, crossing over strand X for a short distance. Strands 5 and Y both cross strand 1. Strand 5 is woven under strand 3, but Y is folded backward to the right and under strand 2. This same system of overlays continues down the braid, folding and passing back and forth in the same sequence (although not under and over the same number strands). Many different overlays can be used. The more strands in the braid, the greater the possibilities.

6-41. A pattern for plaiting based on a weave of the Kamarakoto Indians of Venezuela.

6-42. A plaiting pattern adapted from a macrame design by Joan Michaels Paque, whose source of inspiration was a plaiting pattern!

6-43. An adaptation of a Samoan plaiting pattern.

6-44. A pattern used by the Maoris of New Zealand.

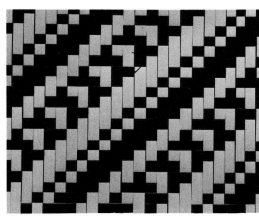

6-45. Another Maori plaiting pattern.

6-46. A Kamarakoto plaiting pattern.

Patterned Weaves

Who knows how many patterns can be made by weaving one set of elements at right angles to a second set? So far in this chapter we have considered only the over-one-under-one plain weave. A few of the many patterns that are found on basketry are illustrated in figures 6-41 through 6-51.

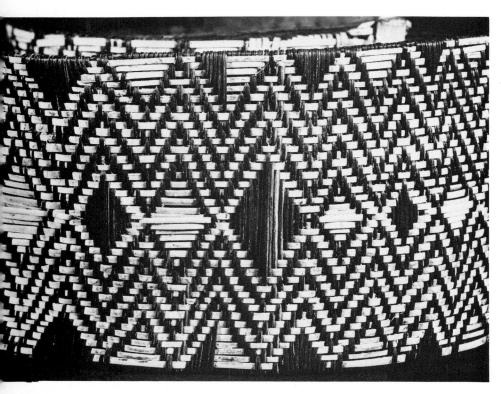

6-47. A belt from Kup, New Guinea, plaited with natural materials over a strip of bark (see figure 7-47). (Courtesy of the American Museum of Natural History, New York)

6-50 and 6-51. A helmet-style hat from Luzon, the Philippines. At the center top, the strands are interlaced at right angles; however, as the hat is formed they come to intersect at an oblique angle. (Courtesy of the American Museum of Natural History, New York)

(Left) 6-48. Plaiting covers two sticks: the longer one is a hair ornament; the shorter, a nose ornament. Both are from Malaita, Solomon Islands. (Courtesy of the American Museum of Natural History, New York)

(Right) 6-49. Plaiting at an oblique angle—a Kamarakoto pattern that appears to be a simple interlacement at first glance.

6-52. Diagonals added to a plain-weave structure.

6-53. A plaiting technique of the Cayapa Indians of Ecuador. Without the diagonals this interlacement would not hold together.

6-54. Diagonals were added to an under-three-over-three twill. A technique of the Kamarakoto Indians of Venezuela.

6-55. A diagonal was added to a plain weave with spaced pairs of strands in this Kamarakoto plaiting design.

6-56. Spaced pairs of diagonals were interlaced in three directions. This is also a Kamarakoto design.

6-57. An open hexagonal weave that is frequently used for snowshoes.

6-58. Extra strands added to the basic pattern in figure 6-57. This pattern originated with the Cayapa Indians.

6-59. Another Cayapa Indian technique.

THREE-ELEMENT PLAITING

Patterned Weaves

Plaiting elements in three directions produces patterns that range from very simple to extremely complex. Figures 6-52 through 6-57 are relatively simple structures. The structure becomes more complex when extra strands are added, as in figure 6-58. The interlacement of figure 6-59 is the same as figure 6-57, except that the number of strands has been doubled in one direction.

6-61.

6-60. A knife in a basketry sheath from Bagabo, Mindanao, the Philippines. (Courtesy of the American Museum of Natural History, New York)

A three-element plaiting that looks similar to the pattern in figure 6-59 was used for the knife sheath in figure 6-60. It is apparent in the reproduction of the pattern in figure 6-61 that the diagonal wefts were woven in an over-one-under-three twill.

Braids

The Maoris of New Zealand have developed a four-strand braid in which the elements go in three directions as the work progresses:

Strands 1 and 2 are woven into strands 3 and 4 at right angles (figure 6-62).

Strand 1 moves to the right, crossing over strands 2 and 3 and under strand 4. Then it changes direction and goes to the left over strand 4 and under strand 3 (figure 6-63).

Strand 4 (on the upper right in figure 6-63) changes direction from right to left. It passes over strands 1 and 3 and under strand 2, then changes direction again and goes over strand 2 and under strand 1 (figure 6-64).

Strand 2 repeats the same interlacement made by strand 1 in figure 6-63, and strand 3 is woven across from right to left in the same manner as strand 4 in figure 6-64. Figure 6-65 shows the braid completed this far. The two steps shown in figures 6-63 and 6-64 are alternated to continue the braid. The strand on the far left is woven across first, then the strand on the far right.

Figures 6-66 and 6-67 illustrate a more complex design of three-element plaiting that is attributed to the Kamarakoto Indians of South America.

One more three-element plaiting technique, the Mad Weave, is discussed below. It is handsome and complex, and it has an interesting story. Although it belongs here among the other three-element techniques, it is placed at the end of the chapter — as a post-graduate project for the plaiter.

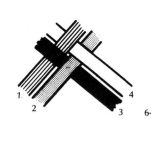

1
2
3
4
6-62.

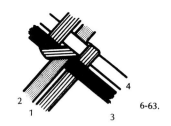

2
1
3
4
6-63.

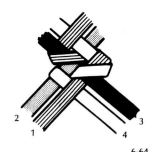

2
1
3
4
6-64.

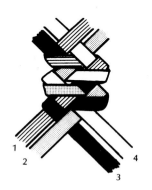

1
2
3
4
6-65.

6-66.

6-67.

FOUR-ELEMENT PLAITING

The traditional pattern for chair caning is four-element plaiting. Paired strands are woven in a spaced plain weave, then diagonals are added in both directions at 45-degree angles, as in figure 6-68. Another pattern with strands in four directions is illustrated in figure 6-69.

MULTIPLE-ELEMENT PLAITING

Plaiting can be done with more than four elements. Elaborate patterns with strands going in several directions can be found in oriental basketry. One example is illustrated in figure 6-70.

6-68. This traditional pattern for chair caning has elements going in four directions.

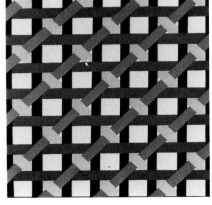

6-70. A complex and beautiful pattern reproduced from a small Chinese basket.

6-69. A Cayapa Indian pattern of spaced plain weave with diagonals in two directions.

THE MAD WEAVE

Anyam Gila, the Mad Weave, is a three-element hexagonal weave that is appropriately named, particularly if you try to reproduce it by looking at an old basket (such as the one in figure 6-71). It would be sacrilege to poke or pry to see where the strands go as they disappear under the surface. An orderly pattern of six-pointed stars is created, but it is a puzzle to reconstruct this without directions.

The first mention of this weave was made by Mrs. L. E. Bland in her article, *Basket-Making at Malacca.* Here she wrote, "it is called *Anyam Gila,* or Mad Weaving. It is very intricate to learn and quite calculated to drive a beginner mad." She says that the female prisoners in the Singapore jail were made to learn the Mad Weave, and "a better punishment could hardly be devised." There are both antique and modern baskets from China, Taiwan, and the Philippines that are made with the Mad Weave.

Mrs. Bland says that baskets were produced in oval, triangular, square, diamond, and hexagonal shapes, and they were often sold in nests of five baskets. The hexagonal shape was the easiest to make and the cheapest. A nest of five baskets took three or four months of steady work to complete and brought four to five dollars.

To make a hexagonal basket in Mad Weave, the plaiting is started at the center inside of the basket with a six-pointed star (figure 6-72). Strands are added on all sides of the star until the bottom reaches the desired size; then the weaving continues up the sides, and a splint hoop is placed at the top. The strands are bent over it and inserted back into the structure, weaving back down the outside and across the bottom, where they are trimmed off. There are six layers of material throughout the basket when it is completed: three that form the initial woven structure and three that are added when the outside strands are inserted back into the weave. As the strands progress down the outside of the piece, some of them are twisted to make a raised pattern (see figure 5-15).

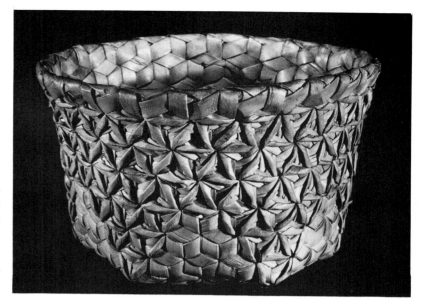

6-71 and 6-72. A basket plaited in Mad Weave from Luzon, the Philippines (see figure 5-15). (Courtesy of the American Museum of Natural History, New York)

To weave the bottom, six strands are interlaced to form the beginning of the center star, as shown in figure 6-73-1. Strands are added on all sides, progressing in succession in a counterclockwise direction, as shown in figures 6-73-2 through 6-73-31. A total of twenty-four strands is used in the example. When the bottom reaches the desired size, no more strands are added. The existing number is sufficient to weave the sides of the basket.

Three shades of gray are used in these illustrations to make the interlacement more easily understood. The six-pointed star that is so apparent in a one-color Mad Weave is more difficult to distinguish when three colors are used, and the color sequence does not continue to make the same pattern when the work starts up the sides of a piece. However, it is helpful to practice the pattern with three colors until the logic of the weave is understood, and it is necessary to illustrate it this way to make it possible to follow.

The strand that is added in each step is marked with an arrow and spaced away from the piece to show the interlacement more clearly. A curved arrow indicates that a strand is crossed over so it is on top before the next strand is added. As the work gets larger, sometimes two strands are crossed to prepare the work for the next weaving.

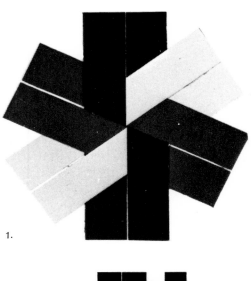

1.

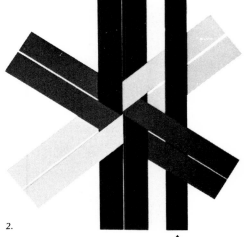

2.

6-73. The sequential steps for plaiting the Mad Weave.

88

3.

4.

5.

6.

7.

8.

9.

10.

11.

12.

13.

14.

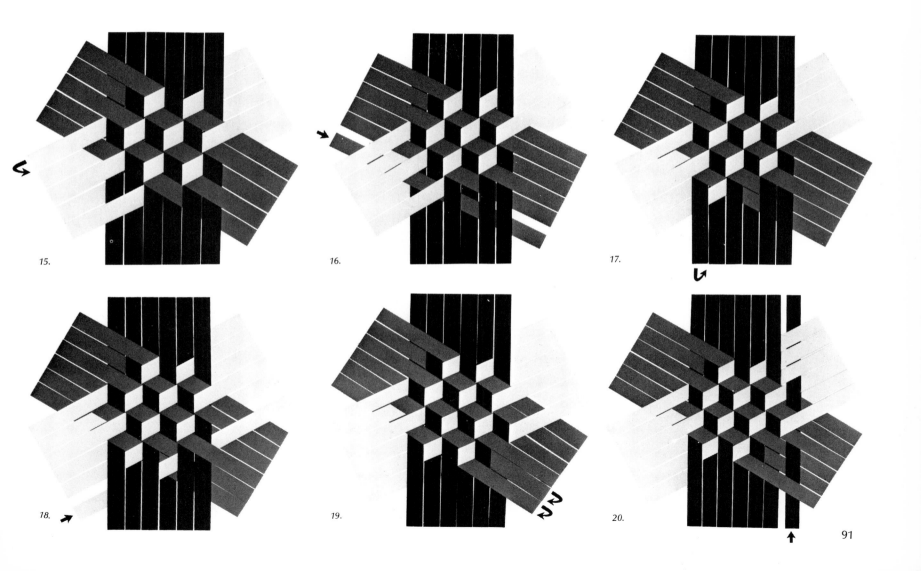

15.

16.

17.

18.

19.

20.

21.

22.

23.

24.

25.

26.

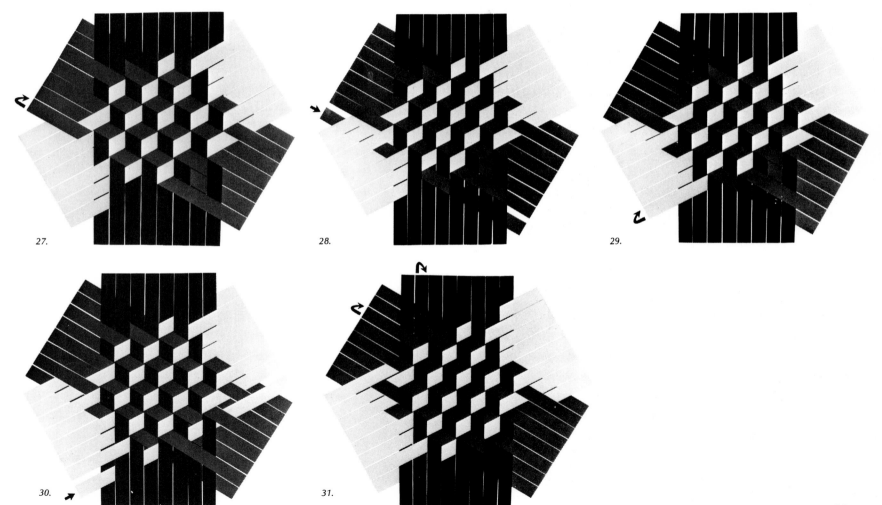

27.

28.

29.

30.

31.

93

To learn the Mad Weave, follow the thirty-one steps given in figure 6-73 (pages 88–93) using three colors of half-inch paper strips at least fourteen inches long. Before starting, look at the structure shown in figure 6-74, where dark arrowed lines show the rows of diamonds that develop when the strips are interlaced. Added strips must continue these tip-to-tip diamond rows, so these rows are clues to enlarging the flat weave beyond the directions given here. For instance, when a strip is added next to strip 17-48, it will go over 6 and 13 (shown with the dotted lines on figure 6-74), and thus continue the rows of diamonds going from lower left to upper right. (This is not meant as complete directions for this strip, but an explanation of the logic of the pattern.)

The directions for moving from horizontal base to vertical sides of a Mad Weave structure continue from step 31 of figure 6-73. Adjust all paper strips so they fit together snugly, number them as shown in figure 6-74, then draw the lines shown in this diagram on the practice piece. These lines show where the strips of the base turn from horizontal to vertical to make a three-dimensional hexagonal shape. For this practice piece, it helps to tape the strips in place along the drawn lines, keeping the tape within the hexagonal base so it will not interfere with the strands when they move to a vertical position. For easy reference when following directions, it will help if the numbers at the ends of the strips are also written near to and outside of the drawn hexagon, as shown in figure 6-74. (On this flat diagram, some numbers are not very near the hexagonal outline. On your practice piece, you can move overlapping strips and mark the numbers nearer the hexagon.)

To begin the vertical turn, hold the side of the work with the lines and tapes toward you (the tape and lines will be on the outside bottom of the completed form). Along the drawn lines, fold away from you and crease each group of strips. Some strips will fold back on themselves, others will have diagonal folds. Do not fold the strips beyond the drawn lines on any of the sides. When all folds are made, the piece will become a wild confusion of ends. The color sequence of the base will not continue on the sides; however, with some patience, the ends can be sorted out and the interlacement continued.

So far, the Mad Weave has been flat, and within the pattern are six-pointed stars. See figure 6-75 where the center star of the base has been emphasized with heavy lines. The stars are difficult to see when color is involved, but they are easy to identify in a one-color piece. Instead of six-pointed stars, five-pointed stars are worked at each corner of the bottom hexagon, and it is the reduction from six- to five-pointed stars that causes the plaiting to turn from horizontal to vertical.

With the base held so the strips are folded away from you, the corners are numbered clockwise one through six, and the plaiting of each strip begins on the line where the strip is folded. Four strips at each corner are interlaced first. To

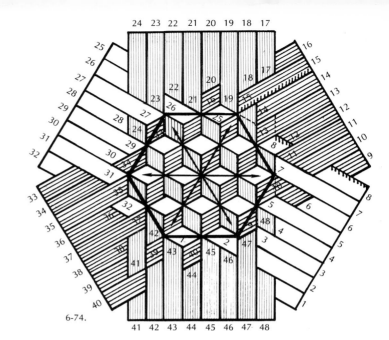

6-74.

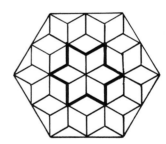

6-75.

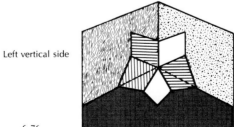

Left vertical side   Right vertical side

6-76.

Base (horizontal)

94

begin, find the corner with strips 8-R (R means the strip moves to the right), 15-R, 25-L (L means the strip moves to the left), and 18-L. (U means that the strip is upright.)

The first two strips that are interlaced in the directions are 8-R and 15-R, and they move to parallel positions when the strips are folded. In figure 6-74, the crosshatched edge of 15-R meets the crosshatched edge of 8-R. Now follow the interlacements as they continue:

1 8-R goes under 18-L, 14-U, 13-U, then over 17-L, 12-U, 10-L.
   15-R goes under 25-L, 20-U, 19-U, then over 18-L, 17-L, 14-U.
   25-L goes over 15-R, 19-U, 20-U, then under 16-R, 21-U, 23-R.
   18-L goes over 8-R, 13-U, 14-U, then under 15-R, 19-U, 16-R.

2 48-R goes under 10-L, 6-U, 5-U, then over 9-L, 4-U, 2-L.
   7-R goes under 17-L, 11-U, 12-U, then over 10-L, 6-U, 9-L.
   17-L goes over 7-R, 11-U, 12-U, then under 8-R, 13-U, 15-R.
   10-L goes over 48-R, 5-U, 6-U, then under 7-R, 11-U, 15-R.

3 40-R goes under 2-L, 46-U, 45-U, then over 1-L, 44-U, 42-L.
   47-R goes under 9-L, 4-U, 3-U, then over 2-L, 46-U, 1-L.
   9-L goes over 47-R, 3-U, 4-U, then under 48-R, 5-U, 7-R.
   2-L goes over 40-R, 45-U, 46-U, then under 47-R, 3-U, 48-R.

4 32-R goes under 42-L, 38-U, 37-U, then over 41-L, 36-U, 34-L.
   39-R goes under 1-L, 44-U, 43-U, then over 42-L, 38-U, 41-L.
   1-L goes over 39-R, 43-U, 44-U, then under 40-R, 45-U, 47-R.
   42-L goes over 32-R, 37-U, 38-U, then under 39-R, 43-U, 40-R.

5 24-R goes under 34-L, 30-U, 29-U, then over 33-L, 28-U, 26-L.
   31-R goes under 41-L, 36-U, 35-U, then over 34-L, 30-U, 33-L.
   41-L goes over 31-R, 35-U, 36-U, then under 32-R, 37-U, 39-R.
   34-L goes over 24-R, 29-U, 30-U, then under 31-R, 35-U, 32-R.

6 16-R goes under 26-L, 22-U, 21-U, then over 25-L, 20-U, 18-L.
   23-R goes under 33-L, 28-U, 27-U, then over 26-L, 22-U, 25-L.
   33-L goes over 23-R, 27-U, 28-U, then under 24-R, 29-U, 31-R.
   26-L goes over 16-R, 21-U, 22-U, then under 23-R, 27-U, 24-R.

Now that the six corners are plaited, there will be no more five-pointed stars. The piece still looks like a wild confusion of ends, but it will begin to become a

6-77. A tour de force in Mad Weave by Ann Meerkerk. The material is leather lacing, and since this lacing is thicker in proportion to its width than most materials used for this technique, the layers of the weave are more evident than usual.

pattern with the next steps. If it is difficult to keep the strips in place as you work, use paper clips to hold them temporarily.

To continue, start again at corner 1:

Strip 15-R becomes a diamond when 19-U and 13-U go over it.

Strip 17-L has previously gone under 13-U and 15-R; now it goes over 14-U and 16-R.

Strip 13-U (right of 15-R) must have a strip moving left to form a diamond, so strand 10-L comes from under 8-R, then goes over 12-U, 13-U, and then 14-U.

With this interlacement of strips 17-R, 14-U, 16-R, 10-L, 13-U, and 15-R, a six-pointed star is beginning to emerge. Now move to the right and weave strips 10-R, 12-U, 15-L, 9-R, 11-U, and 8-L. Continue toward the right, making six-pointed stars. Note that the right-hand diamond of the first star made with 10-L is also the left-hand diamond of the second star. The second and third stars, and all other stars, will have a common horizontal diamond. Vertical sets of stars will also have common diamonds.

Continue working the vertical sides until they are as high as you wish, or the strips become too short to work. The top edge can be finished by turning the strips back on themselves and working them back into the structure, on either the inside or the outside of the piece. See figure 7-83. This diagram shows only vertical strips re-entering the work; however, there are also diagonal strips in the Mad Weave. Unlike the strips in figure 7-83, the diagonal strips do not turn back on themselves. They must fold at an angle to form an even top edge, and then re-enter the work at an obtuse angle.

As if the Mad Weave were not complex enough, additional strips in three more directions can be overlaid and woven into the basic structure. Dark strips on a light ground, as in figure 6-78, produce a pattern of pinwheels. (The black lines were drawn in afterward to make the Mad Weave background more distinct.)

6-78. The Mad Weave with an overlay of dark strands. This pattern was found on a basket of Philippine origin.

BEGINNINGS, FINISHES, AND OTHER DETAILS

Many beginnings, endings, handles, bases, feet, etc. can be used interchangeably for twining, wickerwork, and splintwork, and in some cases for plaiting as well. There are more ways to start and finish a basket than space to document them here, and certainly it would not be possible to record the varieties of handles, bases, feet, lids, knobs, and trimmings that have been used. A representative group of each of these details is included, and these techniques can be used as springboards to individual experimentation. No doubt they will give you ideas for variations of your own, and also, as you notice other baskets, you will find other special techniques to try.

As before, the term *spokes* is used here to refer to the relatively inflexible units forming the structure of the basket, in order to distinguish them from the more flexible *strands* used to hold the former together.

BEGINNINGS

Either an odd or an even number of spokes or strands can be used for a twined basket, but an odd number is preferable for the plain weave of wickerwork and splintwork, so the weave will alternate on successive rows. The four spokes crossed and held in place by lacing an X over the intersection, as shown in figures 7-1 through 7-7, make an excellent small beginning, and the same principle can be used with more than two spokes going in each direction if a larger number is required. When this beginning is used for wickerwork or splint basketry, an extra spoke should be added to make an odd number of ends (dark spoke, figure 7-8). This same principle applies to all the other beginnings that are illustrated; however, spokes can be added in a variety of other ways besides the one shown in figure 7-8.

7-1.

7-2.

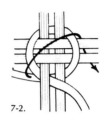

7-3.

7-4.

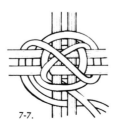

7-5.

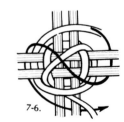

7-6.

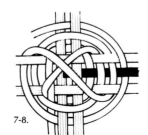

7-7.

7-8.

In all of the illustrations, for the sake of clarity, a limited number of spokes is used, but in most of the examples many spokes could be held together with the same interlacement. Most basketry has either a circular, oval, square, or rectangular shape. Unless otherwise noted, the beginnings illustrated are for circular or square forms. If an oval or rectangular shape is desired, there must be more spokes going in one direction than in the other. For instance, if four horizontal and sixteen vertical spokes are crossed, the shape will be approximately four times as long as it is wide. The shaping that is done as the piece is woven will determine whether it is an oval or a rectangle.

Before you prepare the spokes to begin a piece, it is obviously necessary to determine the proper number of spokes for the particular weave selected. Thus, for plain weave, an odd number is needed; for a twill weave, the number of spokes should be divisible by the number of units in the twill, less the allowance for the twill progression. For instance, if an over-two-under-one weave is to be used, and the twill progression is to move over one spoke in succeeding rows, the number of spokes should be divisible by three, less one subtracted from the total: 30 is divisible by three, and 29 spokes would make the sequence of woven rows step over one spoke in each row, so the weave would follow a twill progression. For an over-three-under-two twill, the progression could move over one, two, three, or four spokes, so there are several choices for the total number of spokes. The span of each weaving repeat (over three, under two) is five spokes, so if we arbitrarily choose five repeats, we would need 25 spokes. In a twill progression that moves over one spoke, the total needed would be 24. To move over two spokes, it would be 23; over three, 22; and over four, 21.

If the bottom of a basket is to be made with a series of spokes that are woven over each other in groups, as shown in figure 7-9, determining the number of spokes is again a problem of multiples. In this illustration, 36 spokes are used, because that number is divisible by 6, 3, 2, and of course 1, for the successive rows: at the center the twining spans six spokes for three rows, then three spokes for three rows, two spokes for three rows, and, finally, single spokes for the last two rows. A beginning of 60 spokes could be woven in successive rows of groups of 5, 4, 3, 2, and 1, because 60 is divisible by each of those numbers.

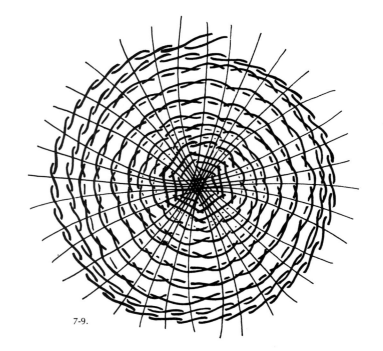

7-9.

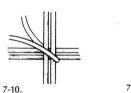

7-10.

7-11.

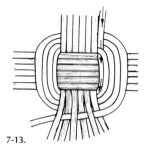

7-12.

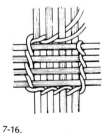

7-13.

One of the simplest beginnings is a single loop over the crossed spokes, as shown in figures 7-10, 7-11, and 7-12. In figure 7-13, two groups, each with six spokes, have been crossed and wrapped. If the same material is used for the spokes and the strands, a length for an additional spoke can be left at the starting end, and this will give an odd number of spokes for plain or twill weave.

Several rows of twining, each loop of the twining enclosing the entire group of vertical or horizontal spokes, hold the crossed spokes together. This interlacement can begin as in figures 7-14 and 7-15. Although the spokes are spaced out in these drawings, they fit together snugly when the twining loops are tightened. In figure 7-16, on the other hand, the spokes are spaced, because the crossing of the twining strands holds them apart to some extent. The method shown in figures 7-14 and 7-15 is the most desirable for a circular form, because the first few rows hold the spokes together firmly, then a row or two of twining separates them, so they begin to radiate into a circular form. The beginning in figure 7-16 is better for a square or a rectangular form.

Wrapping the spokes as shown in figures 7-17 and 7-18 spaces them proportionally, according to the number of wraps between each spoke. This beginning can be used only for four spokes and a square or circular shape, but some variation could probably be devised to accommodate more horizontal or vertical spokes, or both.

7-14.

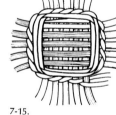

7-15.

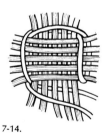

7-16.

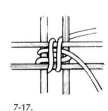

7-17.

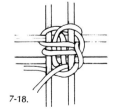

7-18.

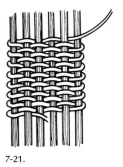
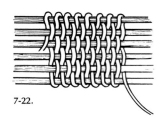

7-21.   7-22.

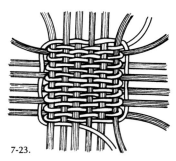

7-23.

7-19 and 7-20. An explosion of color, aptly titled *The Chinese Firecracker*, by Linda Watson. Twined with jute and Canadian and Greek wools over reeds. 15½" high x 15" wide. The detail shows the bottom of the piece, which was twined with the technique shown in figures 7-21 through 7-23.

The bottom of the *Chinese Firecracker* (figures 7-19 and 7-20) is a double layer. To start a piece this way, the vertical spokes are first woven together as a group, as shown in figure 7-21, then the horizontal spokes are woven together in a separate group (figure 7-22). One woven group is placed on top of the other, maintaining the vertical and horizontal positions of each piece, thus causing the unwoven spokes to extend in four directions. The weaving then continues around the four sets of spokes, as in figure 7-23. The remainder of the piece is woven in a single layer, leaving only the square at the beginning as a double layer. One disadvantage of this beginning is that it is bulky, particularly for a small form, and frequently it assumes a rounded shape that causes the completed piece to tip.

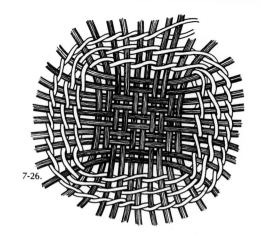

7-26.

7-24.

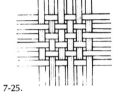

7-25.

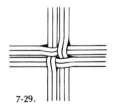

7-27.

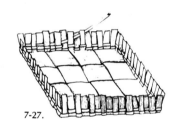

7-28.

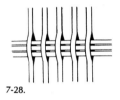

7-29.

7-30.

7-31.

The beginning illustrated in figure 7-24 is related to the feather stitch in embroidery. It moves over three spokes, back two, then crosses itself as it goes to the next loop on the alternate side. Two strands are worked in opposition over the spokes, and an attractive interwoven pattern covers the intersection. The strands in this illustration span two spokes in each loop, but they could span more or less than two, providing each spoke is bound into the structure.

Checkerwork with splints or reeds makes an excellent beginning (figure 7-25). Frequently the entire bottom of a basket is woven this way, and then another technique is used to weave the sides. Paired plain weave (figure 7-26), twill, or, more rarely, a patterned plaiting design have also been used for beginnings. When a checkerwork base of wide splints is used, the splints may be split into many vertical spokes for the sides (figure 7-27). Horizontal crossing strands may be inserted into reeds that have been split lengthwise (figure 7-28). This is referred to as a *slath* beginning by some basketmakers. In *Swedish slath,* pairs of strands are inserted into pairs of spokes going in the opposite direction, alternating the penetration (figure 7-29). According to Dorothy Wright (in *A Caneworker's Book for the Senior Basketmaker*), this technique is not difficult if the interlacement is kept open until all of the strands and spokes are placed in position, then pushed together.

Lacing the spokes together in the manner of a *God's Eye* makes a handsome, more elaborate center. Figure 7-30 shows the beginning of this fastening, which progresses in a clockwise direction with the strand looped behind each group of spokes from the right toward the left. Figure 7-31 shows a small center completed.

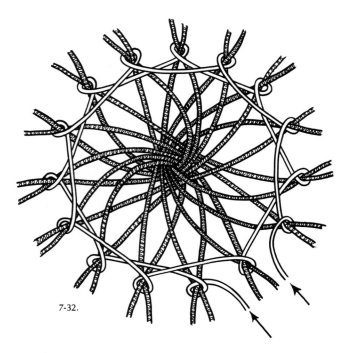

7-32.

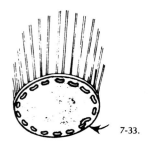

7-33.

7-34. A rattle made of split vines in plain weave (see figures 1-5 and 7-97). They were fastened to a base of hide with holes punched in it to begin the work.

In figure 7-32 thirty spokes are bent around each other and held together with a strand looped around alternate pairs of spokes, encircling the center twice to fasten all of the spokes. Arrows indicate the beginning and ending of the looping strand. One of these ends is concealed in the work, probably by slipping it through an adjacent loop, and the other end continues as a weaving strand. If a twining technique is used, both ends could serve as weavers.

Wood bases of many kinds and shapes can be used to begin baskets. Usually they are plywood (although other rigid materials can be used), and holes are drilled at equal intervals near the perimeter. Each spoke is double the length desired for the piece. One end is inserted through a hole, and the other is inserted in an adjacent hole, which leaves the bend of the spoke on the underside of the base (figure 7-33). If all spokes are attached to the base by doubling, an even number of spokes will result. For plain weave and some twill weaves, an odd number is necessary; a single length of spoke (instead of a doubled one) must be added by inserting one end far enough through a hole to weave it under one of the loops created by a doubled spoke, as shown by the arrow in figure 7-33. If a footing is needed below the plywood, extra strands can be woven into the loops.

When the spokes are not doubled, as in figure 7-35, the ends can be braided or twisted together to make a footing. In figure 7-36, the ends are braided in the following way:

End 1 passes above (on the center side of) ends 2 and 3, below (on the outside of) ends 4 and 5, then toward the center between ends 5 and 6.

End 2 passes above (on the center side of) ends 3 and 4, below (on the outside of) ends 5 and 6, then toward the center between ends 6 and 7. This same sequence is repeated around the base, and the last few spokes are woven into the first ones, continuing the pattern unbroken so the beginning and ending blend together. The ends of the spokes are clipped so they are hidden by the interlacement.

7-35.   7-36.

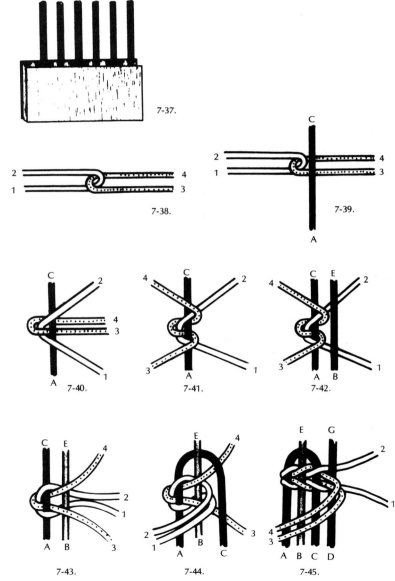

7-37.

7-38.

7-39.

7-40.   7-41.   7-42.

7-43.   7-44.   7-45.

Sometimes it is necessary to hold a series of spokes in place until they are secured by some type of interlacement. Some materials, such as plastic welting cord, can be pinned to a surface like a piece of insulation board. A strip of corrugated cardboard is convenient to slip the ends into to hold them (figure 7-37). If a cylindrical form is to be woven, the ends can be inserted into a piece of cardboard rather than the plywood shown in figure 7-35 and thus held until the weaving supports them sufficiently. Then the cardboard can be removed and the construction of the piece continued.

The method used by the Maoris to start twined fabrics can be adapted to start a rectangular basketry piece. Doubled strands are held in place with countered twining, and both rows of the twining are worked across the piece simultaneously, as follows:

Two weaving strands, 1-2 on the left and 3-4 on the right, are interlocked (figure 7-38).

Strand A-C is placed vertically over strand 3-4 to make a spoke (figure 7-39).

Strand 1-2 is brought to the right over A-C and spaced apart (figure 7-40) so strand 3-4 can be brought between them and to the left (figure 7-41).

Strand B-E is placed over strand 1-2 to make another spoke (figure 7-42).

Strand 3-4 is brought to the right and spaced so strand 1-2 can be brought between it and over strand 3 to the left (figure 7-43).

Strand C is brought across strand 3-4 to make the third spoke (figure 7-44).

The steps shown in figures 7-40 and 7-41 are repeated; then strand D-G is added to make the fourth spoke (figure 7-45).

Strand E becomes the next spoke, and a new strand is added to make every other spoke thereafter, alternating with the end of a previous spoke in the manner of C in figure 7-44.

A B C D E F G H   7-46.

7-47. Detail of a plaited belt from Kup, New Guinea, which was woven of natural materials and supported by a wide strip of bark (see figure 6-47). It was started by looping strands over a stick and securing them with reversed double half hitches.

INCREASING, DECREASING, AND SPLICING SPOKES

Any work over spokes, whether it is twined or wrapped, a twill or a plain weave, can be increased by adding spokes and decreased by removing them. To add a spoke, the new one is laid beside one of the spokes of a piece. (Tapering it makes it blend into the piece more smoothly.) Several rows are woven over the two spokes, treating them as one, and then the added one is woven over individually, taking its place among the other spokes. Figure 7-48 illustrates two spokes added this way, one on each side of a spoke. Spokes can be added by folding them and holding them in place with a row of twining if the material is flexible, as shown in figure 7-49.

Decreasing the work reverses this process. At the point where the decreasing is to begin, two spokes (or more, if the amount of reduction is to be greater) are woven as one for a few rows, then one of the two is cut off, and the subsequent rows are worked over the remaining spoke.

Changing the size of the weaving strands can be used as a method of increasing and decreasing the size of the work also. In figure 7-50, the same number of spokes was used throughout, but the twining was started near the coiled lid with narrow cord, then a medium-sized material was used for several rows, and finally bulky yarn formed the wide bulge. Some of the spokes were removed as the work was reduced at the bottom, and the remaining ones were pulled into the center on completion of the twining at the bottom.

When a weft material runs out in the midst of the weaving, sometimes it is possible to substitute a new strand and overlap the ends or thread them into the reverse side of the work later. If reeds or other thick wefts are being used, it may be necessary to splice them, as shown in figure 7-51. The weaving will hold the spliced ends in some structures, but it is generally safer to glue them.

Figure 7-46 shows a row of spokes that are held together with this technique.

This same technique can be used as a finish on the edge of a completed piece. The row of countered twining is woven across, the ends are looped back so they are hidden under the finished piece, and the scallop of loops forms a decorative edge.

104

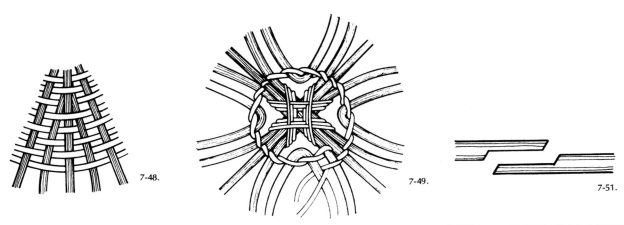

7-48.

7-49.

7-51.

7-50. This dramatic piece was made by Carol Shaw with a combination of techniques and materials. The lid was coiled (see figure 3-115), and the rest of the piece was twined. The spokes and upper part of the twining are heavy linen; the darker twining yarn is jute. The feathers and beads (which are oven-dried carrots) were added after the work was completed. (Courtesy of Helen Richards)

BORDERS AND OTHER FINISHES

To finish a piece of wickerwork, the spokes are usually interwoven into themselves in a pattern and then either inserted back into the work or trimmed short, usually on the reverse side. Many patterns, from very simple to moderately complex, are possible. Variations of spacing and the size of the loops left in the interlacement alter the appearance of borders with identical structures.

An easy way to learn the interlacement of a border is to insert a series of spokes into corrugated cardboard, as in figure 7-37. Any of the materials mentioned previously as suitable for spokes can be used. Number the spokes to correspond with the illustrations, and then follow the directions. They are not as difficult as they appear.

Scalloped Border (figure 7-52)
Spoke 1 goes behind spoke 2 and down into the work beside spoke 3.

Spoke 2 goes behind spoke 3 and down into the work beside spoke 4, etc.

Interwoven Scallop (figure 7-53)
Spoke 1 goes in front of spoke 2, behind spokes 3 and 4, and down into the work beside spoke 5.

Spoke 2 goes in front of spoke 3, behind spokes 4 and 5, and down into the work beside spoke 6, etc.

Interwoven Scallop with Back Trac (figures 7-54 and 7-55)
Spoke 1 goes in front of spoke 2 and behind spoke 3, then backtracks down to its original position. This produces a scalloped edge with a rolled, ropelike effect. Repeat the same sequence: spoke 2 goes in front of spoke 3, behind spoke 4, then back down to its original position, etc.

106

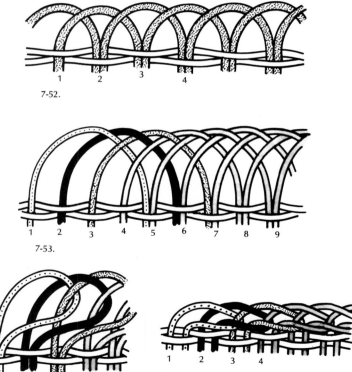

7-52.

7-53.

7-54.

7-55.

Interwoven Scallop with Interwoven Forward Trac (figures 7-56 through 7-59)

If the spokes are pulled down as this border is worked, the scallop will not be pronounced; if the loops are left loose, a scallop with a ropelike twist below it is formed. The border is begun as illustrated in figure 7-56:

Spoke 1 goes behind spoke 2, spoke 2 behind spoke 3, and spoke 3 behind spoke 4.

The next steps, illustrated in figure 7-57, are:

Spoke 1 goes in front of spoke 3, the end of spoke 2, spoke 4, the end of spoke 3, and finally behind spoke 5.

Spoke 4 goes in front of the end of spoke 3, then behind spoke 5.

Continue as illustrated in figure 7-58:

Spoke 2 goes in front of spokes 4 and 5, behind spoke 6, and comes forward between spokes 6 and 7.

Spoke 3 goes in front of spokes 5 and 6, behind spoke 7, and comes forward between spokes 7 and 8.

Spoke 4 goes in front of spokes 6 and 7, behind spoke 8, and comes forward between spokes 8 and 9.

Spoke 5 goes behind spoke 6, in front of spokes 7 and 8, behind spoke 9, and comes forward between spokes 9 and 10.

Spoke 6 goes behind spoke 7, in front of spokes 8 and 9, behind spoke 10, and comes forward between spokes 10 and 11.

The sequence of the interlacement for spokes 5 and 6 is continued. The ends can be clipped short so they are hidden under the ropelike twist, or they can be tucked back into the reverse side by going in front of the spoke on the right and between it and the next spoke (figure 7-59).

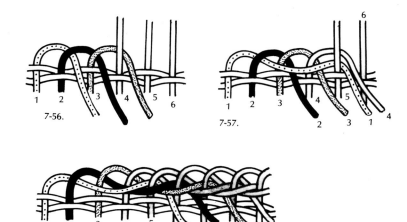

7-56.

7-57.

7-58.

7-59.

Interwoven Scallop, Interwoven Follow-on with Back Trac (figure 7-60)
Follow the same interlacement as shown in figures 7-56 through 7-59;
then the back trac is woven as follows:

After spoke 1 has gone behind spoke 5 (as shown in the previous
directions), it reverses direction and goes in front of spokes 5, 4, and 3,
then returns to the back between spokes 2 and 3.

Spoke 2 reverses around spoke 6, goes in front of spokes 6, 5, and 4,
and returns to the back between spokes 3 and 4.

This sequence is repeated.

After completing a sample of each of the preceding borders, not only
should the principles of scalloping, interweaving forward, and backtrack-
ing be understood, but also the treatment of ends that are brought to the
front, turned to the back, or inserted into the work. Many different
borders are possible by interchanging these elements together with the
variation of using single, doubled, or tripled spokes. For instance, the
border in figure 7-61 is a scallop under two spokes and over two spokes,
all executed with three spokes working as one.

Many variations of interlacing beyond the scallop are possible, and two
examples are given. Figure 7-62 shows a plain weave which goes behind
(or under) one spoke and in front of (or over) the next, and figure 7-63 is
a more complex over-one-under-one-over-one sequence. Some of the
other possible interlacements are:

Over 1 (or 2, or 3), under 1 (or 2, or 3).

Under 1 (2, 3), over 1 (2, 3).

Over 1 (2, 3), under 1 (2, 3), over 1 (2, 3).

Under 1 (2, 3), over 1 (2, 3), under 1 (2, 3).

Going over or under more than three spokes is feasible in some instances also.

108

7-60.

7-61.

7-62.

7-63.

Braided borders make an orderly and frequently a dramatic edge. One example is shown in figures 7-64 through 7-69. The sequence of interlacements is as follows:

Spoke 1 is bent to the right in front of spokes 2 and 3, and spoke 2 goes behind spoke 3 and forward between spokes 3 and 4 (figure 7-64).

Spoke 3 is bent to the right in front of spokes 4 and 5 and goes behind spoke 1 (figure 7-65).

Spoke 4 is bent to the right and paired with spoke 1, then spoke 2 proceeds to the right behind spokes 3, 1, and 4 (figure 7-66).

Spoke 3 moves to the right in front of spokes 1 and 4 (figure 7-67).

Spoke 5 is paired with spoke 2, both go in front of spoke 3, then spokes 4 and 1 move in front of spokes 2 and 5 (figure 7-68).

Spoke 6 is paired with spoke 3, and both go in front of spokes 4 and 1 and behind spokes 2 and 5 (figure 7-69).

In the next interlacement, spoke 1 is dropped on the reverse side of the work, and spoke 7 joins spoke 4 to make the pair. Thereafter, each time a new spoke is brought into the braid, one spoke is dropped at the back, so only two spokes are working together at all times.

If the braid is worked on a circular piece, when the circle is completed and the interlacement of the first few spokes is reached, those parts of the braid that have only single spokes are paired with the remaining ends. When they are all paired and the ends are brought to the reverse side, there should be no break in the pattern to indicate where it starts and where it ends.

A single-spoke edge is not as satisfactory as a double- or triple-spoke braid, because the places where ends are dropped and new ones are worked into the braid are more apparent, and the braid is not as smooth. The more spokes used, the more dramatic the braid.

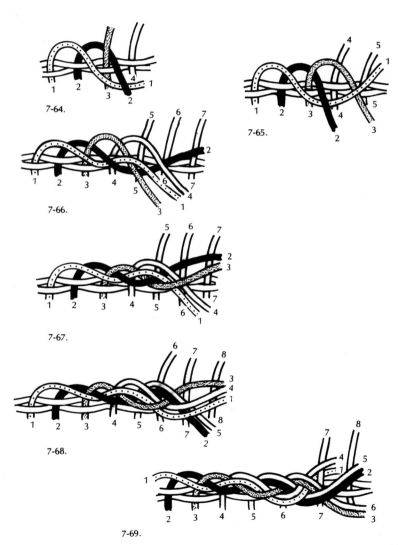

7-64.

7-65.

7-66.

7-67.

7-68.

7-69.

109

7-70. A mixture of wools and sisal were twined over sisal spokes by Carolyn La Belle to make this unusual piece. 6″ high x 6″ in diameter.

7-71.

7-72.

Some twined Indian baskets are woven so firmly that the spokes can be clipped at the edge of the twining, and no extra finish is needed to hold the last rows in place. The same technique was used in the little piece in figure 7-70, but here the weaver left a short length of the sisal spokes beyond the edge of the work and then combed out the fibers to make an unusual finish for her basket.

Frequently on wickerwork, splintwork, or twined and plaited baskets that need reinforced edges, splints are placed on both sides of the spokes, as shown in figure 7-71. The spokes are cut so their ends are even with the top of the splints, and the splints can be lashed in place in one of several ways. In figure 7-71, the semicircular splints are held in place with a simple wrapping or coiling over them and between the spokes. Flat splints are used in figure 7-72, and the crossed lashing holds them in place.

Several different finishes with splints were used on the basket from Luzon in figure 7-73. The splints on the upper edge of the outside piece were covered completely, and the other edges were covered by strips of bamboo cut to fit over them and laced in place with wire. Strips of bamboo held in place by a braidlike finish protect the corners of the interior piece. Directions for this finish are included with the description of figures 3-110 and 3-111.

7-73. A beautifully crafted man's case from Ilokano, Ilokos of North Province, Luzon, the Philippines. (Courtesy of the American Museum of Natural History, New York)

7-74.

7-75. Wood beads are combined with brown and red wool in a small twined piece by Carolyn La Belle. The ends of the spokes are concealed under the stitching on the rim. 6" high x 5" in diameter (at top).

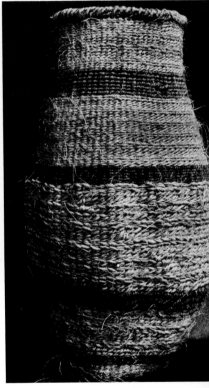

7-76. Stitching over the spokes at the top produces a sturdy rim on this pothanger by Mieke Solari (see figure 1-14).

7-77. The shape of this jar by Clarissa Hewitt was determined partly by the rim, which was created by stitching over the accumulated spokes (see figure 4-18). (Photograph by Bonnie Schiffman)

The spokes can be bent over each other at right angles, all in the same direction (usually to the left), and then held together with some form of wrapping (figure 7-74). As the spokes accumulate in the group, some are dropped out and clipped short, either as the wrapping progresses or after the edge is completed. Usually at least three spokes are kept in the group as it is wrapped. The contemporary baskets shown in Figures 7-75, 7-76, and 7-77 were finished this way, but they were wrapped over many spokes.

A more elaborate wrapping found on a Paiute basket is illustrated in figure 7-78. The spokes are bent to the left and accumulated into a group, and stitches are made between the edge of the work and this group of spokes. The stitching material goes from front to back between two spokes, continues over the top of the group and over itself in a left-to-right direction, loops behind the first spoke at its immediate right, changes direction, and proceeds to the next opening between the spokes, where it goes through from front to back again and repeats the sequence.

7-78.

7-79.

7-80.

7-81.

7-82.

An inverted border can be made with wide splints. They are turned over the top row (or, in some cases, a heavier splint) and inserted back into the weave of the piece, as illustrated in figure 7-83. The spokes are tucked alternately into the front and back sides of the top row. Simple plaited work can also be finished this way in some cases, but it does not produce a very secure edge for the more elaborate plaited patterns.

The decorative finish in figure 7-84 is made so the lower, plaited part of the basket is sandwiched between the horizontal reeds and held firmly, thus making a sturdy seam that will bear the weight carried in the basket.

Imaginative finishes are shown in figures 7-85 and 7-86. No attempt was made to hide the ends in the little hanging sculpture — rather, they were exploited. The piece was started at the bottom, just above the tassel, worked to the area near the top where the feathers are, then part of the spokes continued on to the top, and part of them were brought through the center to form the tassel at the bottom.

7-83.

Often the ends of the spokes are simply bent back into the twining in the manner of the simple scallop in figure 7-79, but there are elaborations on this easy finish too. For instance, another row of twining can be worked over the loops, as shown in figure 7-80. If the twist of the twining in the added row is reversed, the effect is quite different. Extra strands can be added into the top row (figure 7-81) or a row near the top, or a braid can be held in place by a row of twining, as shown in figure 7-82. These last four twined finishes were used on Tlingit Indian baskets.

112

7-84. This burden basket from Borneo (see figure 1-1) has a plaited border.

(Left) 7-85. Braided coconut fiber and feathers were twined in this sculpture by Margaret Wright. 44" long x 7½" wide.

(Right) 7-86. A twined basket with an unusual finish by Annabel Bergstrom. Made of tan and brown raffia, with brown glass beads at the top of the twining. 11½" high; the bottom is 3" square.

(Left) 7-87. Twined feet were added to this coiled bowl by Joaline Stedman (see figure 3-50). (Photograph by Bonnie Schiffman)

(Right) 7-88. Glada Mae Henderson combined coiling and twining and a variety of materials and forms into a successful design. (Photograph by Bonnie Schiffman)

7-89 and 7-90. A shallow rectangular tray supported on four wooden legs. It was plaited of natural fibers by Kamarakoto Indians, Urúyen, Venezuela. The detail shows the corner bracing. (Courtesy of the American Museum of Natural History, New York)

FEET

The ends form the support for the round-bottomed bowl in figure C-1 (page 97). This treatment also fulfilled another requirement; it covered the white plastic welting cord used for the spokes. The artist felt its color would not blend with the gray and burgundy rayon straw used for the weaving, so scalloped or braided edges were ruled out. A rather ordinary shape thus developed into an unusual sculptural piece as the problems of function and materials were solved.

Twined feet were added to the two coiled pieces in figures 7-87 and 7-88. In the latter piece, some of the spokes that form the feet were carried over the top to make a three-part handle-like extension that completes the interesting form. The feet in figure 7-87 continue the graceful lines of the bowl. The feet on both pieces were started at the bottom and made by the technique explained in figures 7-21, 7-22, and 7-23.

The Kamarakoto Indians of Venezuela attached wood legs to a rectangular plaited tray to make the small table shown in figure 7-89. Figure 7-90 is a detail of the lashing used on each post and corner support.

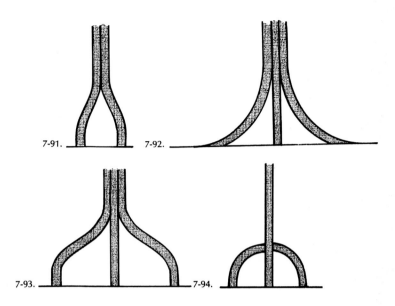

7-91.   7-92.

7-93.   7-94.

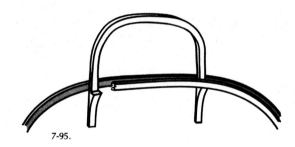

7-95.

HANDLES

Handles have to support the weight placed in a container, so they should be sturdy and securely attached to the piece. Some common shapes that are created where handles attach to baskets are shown in figures 7-91 through 7-94. Splints around the outside rim will hold a notched handle, like the one in figure 7-95, if they are lashed together firmly. One method of securing a handle is to drive a small wood peg through the handle below the splints, as shown in figure 7-96. A peg alone, without splints, will hold a handle below a wickerwork edge. The peg is trimmed off so it does not protrude beyond the work.

The handles for a basket can be made from the spokes used for the basket itself. Allow a few extra-long spokes on opposite sides for the handle. One long spoke on each side will make a two-spoke handle, or two or more spokes from each side can be used to make a sturdier handle. When the body of the basket is completed, these long spokes are bent over the top and crossed. The spokes from the right side are inserted into the weaving next to the spokes emerging from the left side,

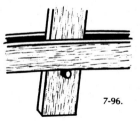

7-96.

7-97. The handle of a Cameroon rattle (see figures 1-5 and 7-34).

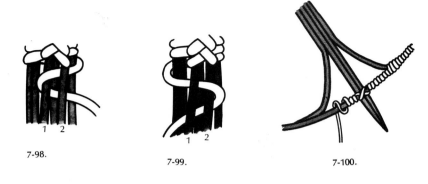

7-98.

7-99.

7-100.

7-101. The God's Eye attachment on the handle adds a colorful pattern to this sturdy basket. (Courtesy of Vivanna Phillips)

and the spokes from the left are inserted into the corresponding space on the right side. The crossed spokes are usually wrapped firmly to complete the handle. Spokes from each of the separate units of the rattle were crossed to form the foundation of the handle in figure 7-97. They were wrapped back and forth, reversing over two reeds at the center front, as shown in figures 7-98 and 7-99. In figure 7-98, the wrapping material comes from behind on the right side. It proceeds from right to left behind reed 2, continues in front of reed 1, and reverses to go behind both reeds. Then it wraps around the entire group, going behind at the right and emerging from the left, as shown in figure 7-99. This time it goes behind reed 1, in front of reed 2, then behind both of them, and continues behind the entire group from left to right, where it emerges in position to repeat the interlacement shown in figure 7-98. This sequence is continued.

The ends of reeds emerging from a handle can be bent parallel to the top of a basket and lashed firmly to one of the top spokes, as shown in figure 7-100. A God's Eye wrapping secures the handle in figure 7-101. (The directions for the God's Eye are given with the description of figures 7-30 and 7-31.)

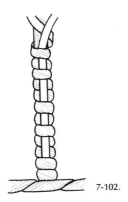

7-102.

Figures 7-102 through 7-109 show some of the many kinds of wrapping that can be used on handles. Some are simply coiled firmly around the handle, with no extra embellishment, like the handles on many oriental teapots. Others add extra materials into the wrapping to form a pattern. The simplest patterned wrapping has an overlay of cane, usually in a contrasting color, running the length of the handle and caught down at intervals with the wrapping material, as shown in figure 7-102. Sometimes more than one strand is worked into the wrapping. The geometric pattern on the African head ring shown in figure 7-103 was created in this manner. Similar patterns can be used to decorate handles.

Wrapping and interweaving over more than one narrow splint running parallel to the handle, as shown in figure 7-104, makes an attractive finish for a handle. Extra strips of cane can be added into the wrapping to form a raised ornamentation. These additional strips of cane are called *listing strands,* and they form a braidlike pattern on the top of the handle, as shown in figures 7-105 through 7-109.

The foundation of the handle may be a sturdy splint or several reeds put together. An extra splint or narrow strip of cane is carried parallel to the foundation material, on top of the reeds and in the center of them. The wrapping material goes in front of this narrow splint on one wrap and behind it on the next. Three extra strands of cane, the listing strands, are threaded behind the narrow splint at the first three intervals where the narrow splint goes in front of the wrapping cord (figure 7-105). When the work begins, these listing strands should be centered under the splint, and they should be long enough to complete the added ornamentation.

7-103. A ring from Africa; it may have been used on the head to help support a burden. The Ethiopian butter bottle has a coiled bottom (see figures 1-11 and 6-2). (Courtesy of Leslie and Fred Hart)

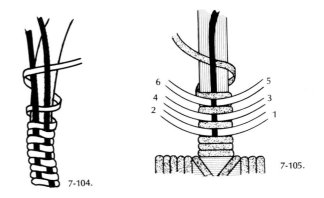

7-104.

7-105.

117

After the three listing strands are inserted, the wrapping strand turns around the center splint, once in front of it and once behind it, as illustrated in figure 7-105. Then end 1 crosses the middle of the handle and goes behind the center splint in a left-to-right direction, while end 2 crosses the middle and goes behind the splint in a right-to-left direction (figure 7-106). The wrapping continues, going in front of the center splint and then behind it on the second wrap. Next, end 3 follows the same path as end 1, but it goes behind the center splint where it is exposed on the top of the last wrapping, as shown in figure 7-107. End 4 follows the same path as end 2, but it goes behind the center splint in the same position as end 3. The wrapping continues in sequence, with a pair of listing strands crossing behind the center splint each time it is exposed (figure 7-108).

If only one listing strand instead of three is added in the same manner and crossed under the center splint each time it is exposed, it will form a series of small Xs on the handle. A raised design with a ropelike pattern can be created with three listing strands interlaced into the center splint in one direction only, as in figure 7-109.

Canes can be twisted or braided for handles. A forked branch makes a sturdy handle for the strainer shown in figure 3-107. Gnarled and twisted roots that have suitable shapes are used on some oriental baskets. The wood develops a soft, lustrous patina from the oil of the hands that carry them. Figure 7-110 illustrates the oak handle of a Nantucket basket, and figures 7-111 and 7-112 show the hinges and closure of the same basket. This Nantucket basket is an excellent example of the importance of these finishing details. Without them a basket would lose much of its distinctiveness. A basketmaker indicates his skill and his respect for his work by his careful attention to such details.

118

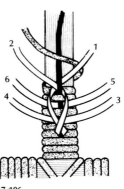

7-106.

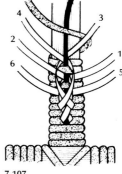

7-107.

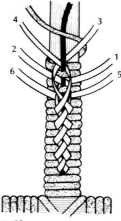

7-108.

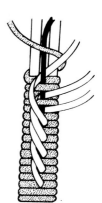

7-109.

7-110, 7-111, and 7-112. A carved ivory button and washer (left) hold the handle in place in an elegant manner on this Nantucket basket. Two loops (above) form a simple, sturdy hinge. The closure (below) is a wrapped loop held in place with a carved ivory pin and eye (see figure 1-13).

8 SOME UNUSUAL TECHNIQUES

8-1. The bottom of a basket from Bangladesh (see figure 1-6).

At first glance, the basket from Bangladesh in figure 8-1 is a puzzle, because the only exterior indications of how it is held together are the supporting strands that go across the outside, and they would not be sufficient to hold coiled reeds such as these in place. Careful examination of the photograph reveals two slight humps running from the center to the rim on the right side of the basket. These bumps are caused by splints that bisect the round canes of the basket in the manner shown in figure 8-2. The canes are spaced apart in the drawing to show how the splints go down through the basket invisibly. Many such ribs keep the canes that form the basket in place.

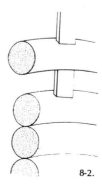

8-2.

120

8-3. A head decoration from Rio Lampaya, Campa. (Courtesy of the American Museum of Natural History, New York)

8-4 and 8-5. A feather and palm-leaf headdress from Vaupés/Caquetá, Colombia and Brazil. The detail shows how stitching near the lower edge holds the two layers of splintwork together. The feathers are inserted between the layers. (Courtesy of the American Museum of Natural History, New York)

Sewing thread was woven over reeds to form a checkerboard design on the head decoration in figure 8-3. On the brim, the reeds were laced together with twining.

A headdress from Brazil, shown in figures 8-4 and 8-5, has an unusual structure. Figures 8-6 and 8-7 show how the four splints are spaced and wrapped with fine strands, forming the skeleton over which flat, flexible strips are laced. This same technique, in much smaller scale, is found in the quillwork of the Blackfoot Indians of central North America.

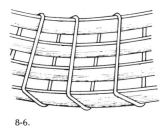

8-6.

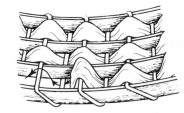

8-7.

In the basket in figures 8-8 and 8-9, two rows of open interlacement contrast with the solid wood bottom to make a handsome and useful accessory. The row of pattern that is next to the base is a repetition of figure eights plaited back into themselves as they are worked from side to side. The outermost border is interlaced in four turns around the basket: the succession is illustrated in figures 8-10 through 8-13. First, a pair of fine reeds is looped (figure 8-10). On the second turn around the basket, the same pattern is interlaced with the first round so the loops fall between the loops of the previous round (figure 8-11). On the third turn, the same pattern is made, but the loops are inverted, and the pair of reeds is interlaced with the previous structure (figure 8-12). The last turn is a repeat of the third round, and again the loops fall between the loops of the previous round (figure 8-13).

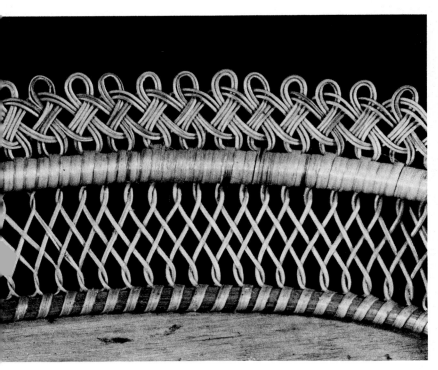

8-8 and 8-9. A basket or tray of unknown origin woven with fine reeds and other vegetal fibers. The bottom is plywood. 13″ long x 9½″ wide x 2½″ high.

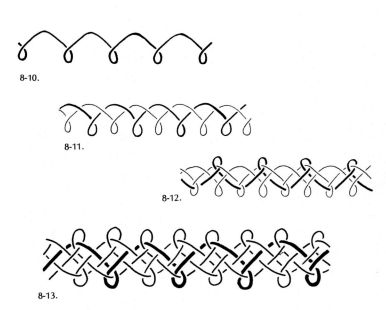

8-10.

8-11.

8-12.

8-13.

123

8-14. A simple structure of folded strands is the basis of this elegant basket. Its origin is unknown. 10″ long x 6½″ wide x 3″ high.

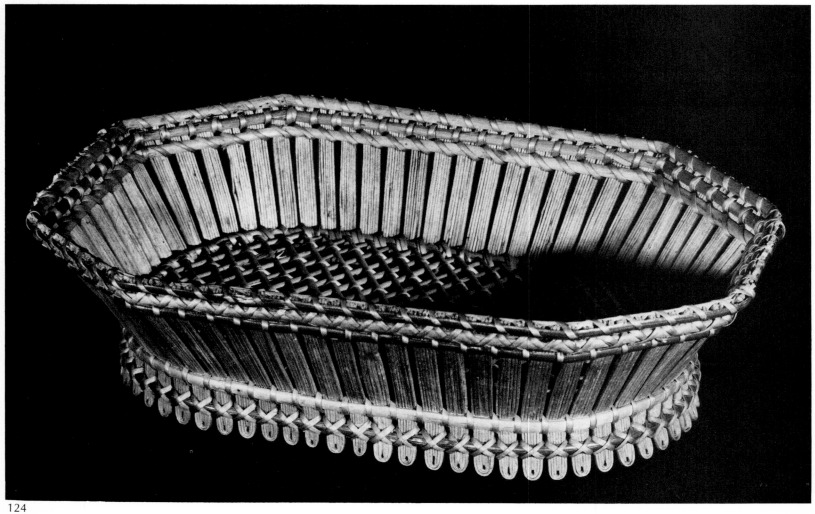

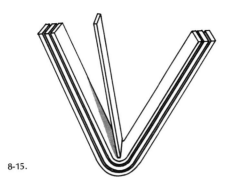

8-15.

A minimum of weaving and stitching was used to construct the basket shown in figure 8-14. The open, hexagonal weave used for the bottom attaches to the reed that forms the oval shape of the base. Each of the groups that form the outside of the basket is made with three small, flat strands folded in half lengthwise. One short strand, half the length of the other three, is placed in the center, the strands are folded as shown in figure 8-15, and the groups are attached to the base with a wide splint that goes over them horizontally. It is stitched to the reed that outlines the base on the inside of the basket. The groups are sandwiched between the two horizontal supports, and the stitching is looped around both of them between each of the groups. For additional support, a second horizontal splint is attached below, near the fold of the upright strands, with a decorative cross-stitch. The top is finished with three more rows of horizontal reeds, and the vertical strands are trimmed flush with the top.

The hanging shown in figure 8-16 suggests yet another way to extend the range of basketry—by combining it with other textile techniques. This piece was made primarily with various basketry and knotting techniques, but the possibilities in this direction are endless (see figures 4-29 and 4-30).

These designs are included because they are difficult to fit into established categories of basketry. Although unusual work is the exception, some basketmakers have been ingenious in their search for different techniques and applications.

It is particularly rewarding when a new method is invented that proves to be useful for a special project. Exploration and experimentation with the basketry techniques described here and with others will create a new awareness that may well lead to new forms, exciting textures, and a new dimension for basketry.

8-16. Techniques of basketry, knotting, and other textile techniques are successfully blended together in this richly patterned hanging by Joan Michaels Paque. (Photograph by Henry Paque)

BIBLIOGRAPHY

The following references were used in the research for this book. Anticipating the desire of serious students of basketry to pursue the subject further, books that have special merit have been annotated. If no comment is made, it can be assumed that the reference offers good information on the subject named in the title.

There are many papers, monographs, and articles in periodicals that contain basketry information but are not listed here: some were not available; some were not used in the preparation of this manuscript. Many of the books that are listed here contain excellent bibliographies, so they are good sources for further exploration.

Adriani, N. and Albert C. Kruyt. *DeBare'e sprekende Toradjas van Midden-Celebes (de Oosi-Toradjas)* [The Bare'e-speaking Toradja of Central Celebes (the East Toradja)]. Second ed. Vol. 1. Koninklijke Nederlandse Akademie van Wetenschappen, Verhandelingen, Afdeling Letterkunde, Nieuwe Reeks, Deel 54, Noord-Hollandsche Uitgevers Maatschappij, Amsterdam, 1950.

Barrett, S. A. *The Cayapa Indians of Ecuador.* Part II, Indian Notes and Monographs No. 40, Museum of the American Indian, Heye Foundation, New York, 1925. The section on plaiting includes a few variations of the hexagonal weave not included in this book.

——. *Pomo Indian Basketry.* The Rio Grande Press, Inc., Glorieta, New Mexico. Originally printed in the publications in American Archaeology and Ethnology of the University of California, Berkeley, Vol. 7, 1908.

—— and E. W. Gifford. *Miwok Material Culture.* Bulletin of the Milwaukee Public Museum, Vol. 2, No. 4, March 1933.

Bland, L. E. *Basket-Making at Malacca.* Journal of the Straits Branch of the Royal Asiatic Society, No. 46, Singapore, Dec. 1906.

Bobart, H. H. *Basketwork Through the Ages.* Oxford University Press, London, 1950.

Bühler-Oppenheim, Kristin and Alfred. *Die Textiliensammlung Fritz Iklé-Huber im Museum für Völkerkunde und Schweizerischen Museum für Volkskunde, Basel* (Grundlagen zur Systematik der gesamten textilen Techniken). Schweizerischen Naturforschenden Gesellschaft Denkschriften, Band LXXVIII, Abh. 2, Gebrüder Fretz AG., Zürich, 1948. This has a German text that includes a limited amount of basketry information, but it is an excellent general reference for textile information and classification.

Buck, Peter H. *The Coming of the Maori.* Whitcombe and Tombs, Ltd., New Zealand, 1952.

——. *Manihiki and Rakahanga.* Bernice P. Bishop Museum, Bulletin No. 99, Honolulu, Hawaii.

——. *Maori Plaited Basketry and Plaitwork.* Transactions of the New Zealand Institute, Vols. 54 and 55.

——. *Plaiting, Arts and Crafts of Hawaii.* Section III, Bernice P. Bishop Museum Special Publication 45, Honolulu, Hawaii, 1964.

——. *Samoan Material Culture.* Bernice P. Bishop Museum, Bulletin 75, Honolulu, Hawaii, 1930.

——. *Twined Baskets, Arts and Crafts of Hawaii.* Section IV, Bernice P. Bishop Museum Special Publication 45, Honolulu, Hawaii, 1964.

Crampton, Charles. *Canework.* The Dryad Press, Leicester, England, 1967.

Emery, Irene. *The Primary Structures of Fabrics.* The Textile Museum, Washington, D.C., 1966.

Gibson-Hill, C. A. *Malay Hats and Dishcovers.* Journal of the Royal Asiatic Society, Malayan Branch, Vol. 24, Pt. I, 1915.

Griswold, Lester and Kathleen. *The New Handcraft, Processes and Projects.* Van Nostrand Reinhold Company, New York, 1972.

Handy, Willowdean Chatterson, *Handcrafts of the Society Islands.* Bernice P. Bishop Museum, Bulletin 42, Honolulu, Hawaii.

Harvey, Virginia I. and Harriet Tidball. *Weft Twining.* Shuttle Craft Guild Monograph No. 28, The Shuttle Craft Guild, Lansing, Michigan, 1969.

Hornell, James. *Primitive Types of Water Transport in Asia: Distribution and Origins.* Royal Asiatic Society of Great Britain and Ireland, Journal, London, 1946.

James, George Wharton. *Indian Basketry* and *How to Make Baskets.* The Rio Grande Press, Inc., Glorieta, New Mexico, 1970. Two books, *Indian Basketry* and *How to Make Baskets,* have been reprinted under one cover.

Kronke, Grete. *Weaving with Cane and Reed.* Van Nostrand Reinhold Company, New York, 1968. If directions for specific baskets are desired, this has an excellent selection of well-designed projects.

Lamb, Dr. Frank W. *Indian Baskets of North America.* Riverside Press, Riverside, California, 1972. Particularly valuable for identification of baskets.

Larsen, Jack Lenor. *Interlacing: The Elemental Fabrics.* Kodansha, New York, 1986

Laufer, Berthold. *Chinese Baskets.* Field Museum of Natural History, Anthropology Design Series, No. 3, 1925. Very little text, many excellent photographs.

Leftwich, Rodney L. *Arts and Crafts of the Cherokee.* Land-of-the-Sky Press, Cullowhee, North Carolina, 1970. Good information on the preparation of materials as well as general data on Cherokee basketry.

Lehmann, Johannes. *Flechtwerke aus dem Malayischen Archipel unter Zugrundelegung der Sammlungen des Städtischen Völker-museums.* Frankfurt am Main Städtisches Völkermuseum, Veroffentlichungen IV, Joseph Baer & Company, Frankfurt am Main, 1912. No information on the text is available, but there are many excellent drawings and photographs of baskets and basketry techniques.

——. *Systematik und Geographische Verbreitung der Geflechtsarten.* Dresden K. Zoologisches and Anthropologisch-Ethnographisches Museum Abhandlunger und Berischte, Band XI, 1970. No assessment can be made of the German text, but there are drawings, two tables of techniques, and a page of photographs that are excellent reference material.

Lismer, Marjorie. *Seneca Splint Basketry.* Office of Indian Affairs Education Division, Indian Handicraft Pamphlets, No. 4, Chilocco Agricultural School, Chilocco, Oklahoma, 1941.

Lothrop, Samuel Kirkland. *Indians of Tierra del Fuego, The Yahagan.* Museum of the American Indian, Heye Foundation, New York, 1928.

Mason, Otis Tufton. *Aboriginal American Basketry.* Rio Grande Press Inc., Glorieta, New Mexico, 1970. Originally printed in the Report of the United States National Museum, 1902.

——. *Anyam Gila (Mad Weave): A Malaysian Type of Basketwork.* United States National

Museum Proceedings, Vol. XXXVI, Washington, D.C., 1909. The only directions for this technique that were found in any literature.

———. *Vocabulary of Malaysian Basketwork: A Study in the W. L. Abbott Collections.* Proceedings of the United States National Museum, Vol. 35, Washington, D.C., 1909.

Mead, Sidney M. *The Art of Taaniko Weaving.* A. H. and A. W. Reed, Sydney, Australia, 1968.

Navajo School of Indian Basketry, Los Angeles. *Indian Basket Weaving.* Dover Publications, Inc., New York, 1971. Directions for making coiled, twined, and plaited baskets, and some information on dyes, wood stains, and polish for baskets.

Nissen, Henry W. *A Field Study of the Chimpanzee.* Comparative Psychology Monographs, Vol. VIII, No. 1 (Serial No. 36), The Johns Hopkins Press, Baltimore, 1931.

Paul, Frances. *Spruce Root Basketry of the Alaska Tlingit.* Education Division, United States Indian Service, Lawrence, Kansas, 1944.

Rossbach, Ed. *Baskets as Textile Art.* Van Nostrand Reinhold Company, New York, 1973.

Roth, Walter Edmund. *Introductory Study of the Arts, Crafts, and Customs of the Guiana Indians.* Johnson Reprint Corporation, New York, 1970. Originally published in 1924 by the Government Printing Office as a paper accompanying the Thirty-Eighth Annual Report of the United States Bureau of American Ethnology to the Secretary of the Smithsonian Institution, 1916–1917. Not only is this an excellent reference for basketry techniques, but also for many nonloom and backstrap loom techniques.

Schneider, Richard C. *Crafts of the North American Indians.* Van Nostrand Reinhold Company, New York, 1974.

Seeler, Katherine and Edgar. *Nantucket Lightship Baskets.* The Deermouse Press, Nantucket, Mass., 1972.

Simpson, George Gaylord. *The Kamarakoto Indians: A Carib Tribe of Venezuelan Guyana.* Manuscript, personal copy of author, *ca.* 1939–1940. This reference can be found in the Human Relations Area File of any library subscribing to that service. The reference needed is HRAF, SS-16, Pemon. Excellent data, drawings, and a detailed classification of basketry.

Speiser, Noemi. *The Manual of Braiding.* Basel, Switzerland, 1983.

Spier, Leslie. *Havasupai Ethnography.* Anthropological Papers of the American Museum of Natural History, Vol. XXIX, Part III, New York, 1928.

Voss, Gunther. *Reinhold Craft and Hobby Book.* Van Nostrand Reinhold Company, New York, 1963.

Wardle, H. Newell. *Certain Rare West-Coast Baskets.* American Anthropologist, Vol. 14, No. 2, 1912.

Weltfish, Gene *Prehistoric North American Basketry Techniques and Modern Distributions.* American Anthropologist, N.S. Vol. 32, Menasha, Wis., 1930.

———. *Problems in the Study of Ancient and Modern Basket-makers.* American Anthropologist, N.W. Vol. 34, Menasha, Wis., 1932.

Whitbourn, K. *Introducing Rushcraft.* Charles T. Branford Co., Newton Centre, Mass., 1969. Many attractive projects.

White, John. *History of a Voyage to the China Sea.* Wells and Lilly, Boston, 1823.

Whiteford, Andrew Hunter. *North American Indian Arts.* Golden Press, New York, 1970. One chapter on basketry has an incredible amount of information in a few pages.

Willoughby, Charles Clark. *Textile Fabrics of the New England Indians.* American Anthropologist, N.S., Vol. 7, Menasha, Wis., 1905.

Winstedt, Sir Richard O. *Papers on Malay Subjects.* Malay Literature, Part II, Kuala Lumpur Federated Malay States Government Press, 1923. Some discussion of basketry including a description of the "Mad Weave." No illustrations of techniques.

Wright, Dorothy. *A Caneworker's Book for the Senior Basketmaker.* The Dryad Press, Leicester, England, 1970.

Wyman, Anne. *Cornhusk Bags of the Nez Percé Indians.* Southwest Museum Leaflet No. 1, Southwest Museum, Los Angeles, California.

INDEX